THE HUMBER STORY

This work is published with the assistance of the Michael Sedgwick Memorial Trust, Coventry City Council and the Peugeot Talbot Motor Company.

The Michael Sedgwick Trust was founded in memory of the famous motoring researcher and author Michael Sedgwick, 1926–83. The trust is a registered charity created to encourage new research and recording of motoring history.

Suggestions for future projects and donations should be sent to the Honorary Secretary, c/o The John Montagu Building, Beaulieu, Hampshire, SO41 7ZN.

Published by Alan Sutton Publishing Limited, an imprint of Sutton Publishing Ltd, in association with the Michael Sedgwick Memorial Trust.

THE HUMBER STORY

1868–1932

A.B. DEMAUS and J.C. TARRING

SUTTON PUBLISHING LIMITED

First published 1989
by Alan Sutton Publishing Limited,
an imprint of Sutton Publishing Limited,
Phoenix Mill, Far Thrupp, Stroud,
Gloucestershire.

Reprinted 1997

British Library Cataloguing in Publication Data

Demaus, A.B.
The Humber story: 1868–1932.
1. Great Britain. Motor vehicle industries.
Humber Ltd, 1868–1932
I. Title II. Tarring, J.C.
338.7'6292.0941

ISBN 0-86299-596-5

Library of Congress Cataloging in Publication Data
applied for

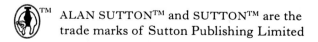
™ ALAN SUTTON™ and SUTTON™ are the
trade marks of Sutton Publishing Limited

Typesetting and origination by
Alan Sutton Publishing Limited.
Printed in Great Britain by
WBC Limited, Bridgend.

Contents

Acknowledgements

The authors express their sincere thanks to the City of Coventry, the Michael Sedgwick Memorial Trust and Peugeot-Talbot, without whose assistance this book would not have seen physical existence. Also to E.M. Lea-Major for his invaluable help in making available Humber archives of the pre-1932 period, and to the many members and former members of The Humber Register for their part in gleaning Humber material over many years.

A.B. DEMAUS
J.C. TARRING

From Pedals to Motors

No study of Humber car production can be placed in perspective without some knowledge and understanding of the growth and activities of the firm prior to its somewhat tentative entry into the world of the automobile in the closing decade of the nineteenth century. The company was not alone, of course, in making the change from cycle manufacture to motor manufacture; indeed, the majority of Britain's pioneer motor-makers trod the same path, though many of them waited a little longer before taking the plunge into motors. Many, too, were destined to fall by the wayside or to be absorbed by other motor manufacturing concerns long before Humber handed over to Rootes in 1932. Fewer still of those which entered the motor industry in the early days, by way of the cycle industry, continued to manufacture cycles, motor cycles and motor cars 'under the same roof' for so long a period as did Humber.

Thomas Humber was born on 16 October 1841, the son of a tailor, Samuel Humber and his wife Lucy, formerly Turton, of Andrew Street in the sub-district of Brightside, Sheffield, Yorkshire. In 1849 the family moved to Hull where Thomas received his education at Salthouse Lane School. In 1854 the family moved again, this time to Nottingham, where young Tom was taken into the employ of a Mr Cross, of Mortimer Street, Nottingham. He was not formally apprenticed to Mr Cross's trade of wheelwright and blacksmith but 'picked it up' well enough for his workmates and his foreman to notice his skill at forging parts for lace-making machinery.

After a year with Mr Cross, Humber moved to join the Bitterley Iron Co., and here too his exceptional skill and talent came to be noticed. Despite his success and the entreaties of his employers for

Thomas Humber, the founder of the firm, mounted on a Humber tricycle of *c.* 1886

him to stay, this was not to be, and of his own volition Humber left them in order to widen the range of his skills and experience. The following years found him moving from employer to employer, in the process taking him back to Hull, and also to Saltley and Wednesbury in the Black Country, after which he returned to Nottingham where he set up on his own in business as a blacksmith.

Immediately prior to launching out on his own he had been employed as chief blacksmith in the business of William Campion at

The Humber 'Spider Bicycle', the first complete bicycle made by Thomas Humber, Nottingham, 1873. Before this he had been making parts for William Campion, who then assembled them

Pace and grace; Beeston Humber 50 in 'Ordinary' of c. 1885

his Roden Street factory in Nottingham, where Campion made and patented improvements in hosiery machinery from 1860 to 1873. The firm also made a chain-stitch domestic sewing machine. William Campion was exhibiting these machines at the Paris Exhibition of 1867 and while in Paris saw, and was much impressed by, the French velocipedes of Michaux type. He bought one and brought it back to Nottingham, asking Thomas Humber to make six sets of copy forgings. P.B. Hamilton's *Life of Thomas Humber* published in 1894 attributes Humber's initial interest in velocipedes to his reading of a letter relating to the Michaux velocipede that appeared in *The English Mechanic* of 4 December 1868. However, several sources agree that the crucial visit to Paris was in 1867, though these accounts do differ in some details. It is likely, therefore, that such influence as the article in *The English Mechanic* may have had on the future course of Humber's career and on the founding of his cycle business was confirmatory rather than inspirational.

Thomas Humber's early machines were made in a shed at the back of his house, 65 Northumberland Street, Nottingham, and were much akin to the French Michaux velocipede but he was always seeking to improve and perfect his products. By 1871/2 his 'Spider Bicycle' machines were already foreshadowing the graceful high-wheeled 'ordinary' that a later generation mischievously dubbed the 'Penny-Farthing'. Never what might be termed a publicity seeker, Thomas Humber, in his early years as a cycle-maker, seems only to have relied on personal recommendation for the advertisement of his machines; yet this was good enough to cause him to seek larger premises at 29A Stretton Street, Nottingham, in 1870 and to move again to Queen's Road in 1875. He did not issue his first catalogue (or, more correctly, price-list) until 1873.

Surprisingly, his early machines were not known as 'Humbers'. In the ensuing few years after the move to Stretton Street, Humber had steadily improved his machines from the clumsy Michaux-type velocipede to the more graceful and lighter 'Spider Bicycle'. Such was the name given to them in Humber's very first published price-list of 1873, in which the solitary illustration of Humber's machine was thus captioned. Nowhere in the text or in the several testimonials is the word 'Humber' applied to the machines, but only to Thomas Humber in person. Some authorities credit that famous racing man and aristocratic Cambridge undergraduate the Hon. Ion Keith-Falconer with the application of the name 'Humber' to the machines, but Keith-Falconer did not enter Trinity College, Cambridge until the Michaelmas Term of 1874, some six years at least after Thomas Humber had produced his first machine.

A testimonial carried by Humber's first price-list came from one F. Cooper of The White Bear, High Street, Sheffield, a keen racing man who had already achieved a number of racing successes on Humber's machines. Fred Cooper was to play a major and significant part in the expansion of the firm. With a Nottingham man, Thomas Rushforth Marriott, Cooper went into partnership with Thomas Humber whose business had now grown large enough to warrant the bringing into existence of the firm of Humber, Marriott & Cooper. The growth of the business had already required another move from Stretton Street to larger premises in Queen's Road, Nottingham, in 1875, and three years later Humber, Marriott & Cooper moved four miles out of the city to new premises at Beeston.

Marriott had joined Humber in 1875, the firm trading as Humber & Marriott, then, in 1877, when Cooper joined the partnership, as Humber, Marriott & Cooper, just a year before the move was made to Beeston. Thomas Humber continued to devote himself to the practical side of manufacture, Marriott to the business side and Cooper, with his splendid reputation as a racing man, opened up a London branch, occupying a house in Lillie Road near the Brompton Cemetery, thus greatly widening the reputation of the firm which had hitherto been confined to more northerly parts.

All this period was one of intense growth and technical development which, allied to the numerous racing successes achieved by riders using Humber machines, laid the sure foundations of the firm's high reputation for quality in every respect. Until the move to Beeston, Humber had not made any attempt to cater for the growing potential market for machines other than 'Spider Bicycles' or

Robert Cripps, whose racing successes on Humber tricycles of this type led to the name 'Cripper' being applied to them, is seen here on a Humber 'Cripper' of *c.* 1884

A tricyclist with a later pattern of Humber 'Cripper' of *c.* 1887

A country outing for a sartorially-elegant gentleman and his Humber tricycle

'Ordinaries', as they eventually became known, but now he turned his attention to tricycles, a field in which he was soon to build a reputation as high as that of his two-wheelers. Thomas Humber had little personal interest in acquiring money, but his two partners could see that the potential was great and parted company amicably from Humber. They set up together as wholesalers of cycles, by so doing causing a most confusing situation. Thomas Humber had taken no steps at the time Marriott and Cooper left the partnership to protect his designs, patents, or the use of his Humber name on other machines. His somewhat naive attitude to the realities of commerce was to cause much subsequent difficulty. Having left the partnership, Marriott and Cooper marketed 'Humber' cycles of their own, these being produced for them by Dan Rudge of Wolverhampton. Having failed legally to prevent Marriott and Cooper's continuance of this practice, Thomas Humber took to naming his machines 'Genuine Humber' (those other than Marriott and Cooper were quite happy to cash in on the reputation of the genuine article) and when Thomas Humber was joined in partnership by Thomas H. Lambert in 1885

This 1896 Coventry Humber Model B Roadster, frame No. 39592, still survives in appreciative ownership in New Zealand. The front wheel is of 30 in diameter

the use of the term 'Beeston Humber' was also — perhaps by way of distinguishing mark — one that was to become synonymous with the highest quality.

It was Lambert who introduced to the company one Martin D. Rucker, an athletic and ambitious young man who had turned his back on the family business of shipbroking and had set up as a cycle-maker in Bethnal Green. This venture failed and he was bankrupted, but the lucky introduction by Lambert to the Humber firm set him on the road to success. Shortly, he became London Manager at Humber's Holborn Viaduct branch (the successor to Fred Cooper's depot in Lillie Road), and before long he rose to become Humber's General Manager. A dashing, extrovert, sporting fellow, always said to be good company, he had expensive tastes and aspirations. He liked to live to the limit of his means, or even beyond, and was described by a contemporary who knew him well over many years as being 'recklessly extravagant'.

J.E. Young of Glasgow, exemplified the racing man and his racing tricycle with his sparkling Humber Direct Steerer

Freed from the autocratic restrictions imposed by old Tom Humber when the latter retired in 1892, something of Rucker's extravagance entered into his conduct of the company's affairs. In the actual production of cycles the firm embraced a number of novelties of very dubious value, one of which was subsequently described by a contemporary expert in cycling affairs as 'the greatest fraud ever foisted on the public'. In his conduct of the company's affairs, Rucker, as General Manager, came strongly under the influence of one of the most shameless entrepreneurs of the period, E.T. Hooley. Hooley certainly had a flair for making money and successfully floated numerous companies. But, as has been pointed out, the climate in the cycling industry at this time provided an ideal

area for speculation. Humber & Co. Ltd., backed by Hooley, promoted subsidiary companies in the USA, Russia, Portugal, Denmark and Sweden in addition to a very sizeable 'depot' of almost factory proportions in Paris. With its British works at Beeston, Wolverhampton and Coventry, Humber's total output put it firmly among the leaders of the world's cycle-makers. By this time Beeston Humbers enjoyed a first class reputation.

But it was too good (or bad, depending on how you looked at it) to last, for Hooley's web of financial entanglements and flotations finally fell about his ears and in 1898 he was bankrupted. The adverse publicity attending this and the revelations that came to light, cast rumours of corruption on the activities of many prominent men in the cycle trade, Humber men among them, and in particular Hooley's close friend and would-be emulator, Martin Rucker, Humber's General Manager.

All this brought about a state of alarm and unease in the cycle industry in which Hooley's flotations had been so prominent. It also brought about the dismissal of Rucker and the entire Humber directorate. The new board was faced with having to make drastic economies and, more particularly, to restore confidence among its shareholders. Further disaster had come in the form of a calamitous fire at the Coventry Works in July 1896. By virtue of much goodwill and the cooperation of other Coventry concerns and, in particular, the almost superhuman efforts of Walter J. Phillips, a new factory of much-increased capacity was built in record time. How fortunate this proved to be became apparent when the Hooley backruptcy disclosures forced remedial action which involved the closing down of the company's overseas factories and those at Wolverhampton.

A rare, possibly unique, survivor in the form of the American Humber, made by Humber & Co. (America) Ltd. at its factory at Westboro', Mass. This example is frame No. 15910 and dates from *c.* 1896

Humber became interested in the 'new-fangled' autocars in 1896 through the influence of another financier of Hooley's ilk, Harry John Lawson, who, like Hooley, was a friend of Rucker's. (Rucker seems to have had a fatal fascination for flashy high-living characters of dubious propriety.) Unlike Hooley, Lawson did have practical experience in the cycling industry, though even in his early days he was not averse to making extravagant claims that could not be subsequently substantiated. As a man of vision, however, he could appreciate the enormous possibilities of the dawning motor age and he set about achieving a complete monopoly of motor manufacturing in Britain. He formed and registered the British Motor Syndicate, and bought up the Daimler patent rights for England from F.R. Simms and formed the British Daimler Company. His British Motor Syndicate then set about buying as many patent rights as possible, including those of a somewhat eccentric American, E.J. Pennington.

Pennington was possessed of a most persuasive plausibility and had some very strange notions of what motor vehicles should be, the majority of his patents being highly impractical. Again, through the

A Beeston Humber dismantled to show the 'Brazeless Joints' (patented in 1896). This type of frame was catalogued until 1908

Rucker connection, Humber & Co. Ltd. found itself saddled with licenses from the British Motor Syndicate to build cars under the Pennington patents. It was not until 1900 that the company was re-formed as Humber Ltd., after the shake-up that followed the Hooley case and the dismissal of Rucker and the directorate of the company, that Humber finally cast loose from the Lawson influence and the unlikely Pennington patents.

The new Managing Director, Edward A. Powell, was faced with restoring the confidence of the trade and the public in Humber's policies and image, as well as cutting down and rationalizing on the extravagances of the Rucker/Hooley era. The result of this policy was the formation of a new company, Humber Ltd., in 1900. The cycle boom of the late 1890s was over, some degree of recession had occurred in the cycle trade and the new motor cars were on the horizon. Edward Powell's task was a formidable one. The two Wolverhampton factories were closed and the majority of Humber's overseas subsidiary companies (all of which had been wholly or partly Hooley's flotations) were also disbanded. The very wide range of models and options was rationalized while at the same time the surviving models were brought into line with recent developments in free-wheels, better brakes, variable gear options and so on.

Production was now centred on the much enlarged Beeston factory and the new Coventry factory, built with remarkable speed after a disastrous fire in the old works in 1896. The chief architect of this commendable recovery in the face of adversity was Walter Phillips.

By 1906 the company itself could clearly see, to quote from a director's meeting of that year, 'that it would be folly not to

Humber cycles held a pre-eminent reputation on the race tracks. Here a Humber Path Racer of 1896 is posed on Herne Hill race track

HUMBER CHAINLESS SAFETY (BEESTON MAKE).

MADE UNDER ACATENE LICENSE.

TO those riders who do not wish to be troubled with the adjustment of a chain, we have pleasure in presenting this design. It embodies all the salient Humber features, with the addition of the best known method of bevelled gearing, and we have little doubt that it will find many patrons. It can be made to the same specifications as our Nos. 1, 3, 5, 7, and 19 patterns as regards tyres, pedals. gear, handle-bar, &c.

PRICE - - £36.

Humber espoused the so-called 'chainless' development by producing this model under Acatène licence in 1898

recognize that as a pastime for the wealthy cycling was nearly dead, and [the company] could not look for an increase in the sale of Beeston cycles'. By that time the motor car was in the ascendant and cycling had to be content with a lower place in the social order. However, the range of cycles offered remained substantially the same until the outbreak of war in 1914.

When normal production resumed after the war, the range was much reduced and prices much increased by comparison with those pertaining pre-war. Only gradually did a few more models or options creep back into the range, but, as E.F. Johnson, who had joined Humber & Co. Ltd. way back in 1889 as clerk to Martin D. Rucker, and who had survived the latter's fall from grace to continue to serve the company for many years, remarked:

Soon after the war I realized that cycle interests were being grossly neglected and were swamped by the increasing car trade. Increased motor production was demanded and this seemed to occupy all the attention of the Directors. In 1919 I suggested to Edward Powell (the Managing Director) that new directors amongst the cycle staff should be appointed to run the cycle trade only. He was not in favour of a cycle board but promised a cycle committee of management. Unfortunately, a few weeks after, he passed away. His successor knew nothing whatever about cycles and took no interest and the result was that the Humber cycle which had been for years the leading machine in the world for design, quality and finish drifted downwards and lost its identity.

"PEDERSEN" SAFETIES (BEESTON MAKE).

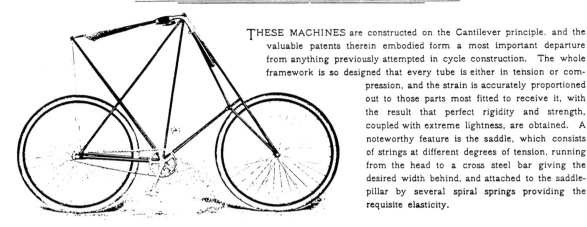

THESE MACHINES are constructed on the Cantilever principle, and the valuable patents therein embodied form a most important departure from anything previously attempted in cycle construction. The whole framework is so designed that every tube is either in tension or compression, and the strain is accurately proportioned out to those parts most fitted to receive it, with the result that perfect rigidity and strength, coupled with extreme lightness, are obtained. A noteworthy feature is the saddle, which consists of strings at different degrees of tension, running from the head to a cross steel bar giving the desired width behind, and attached to the saddle-pillar by several spiral springs providing the requisite elasticity.

The downward drift continued through the 1920s and when the influence of the Rootes brothers on Humber motoring affairs began to be felt it soon became clear that the cycle side of the business had become an embarrassment. No wonder, then, that it was hived off onto Raleigh which continued to use the brand name for many more years.

In this account of the background of the Humber cycle little has been said about the pre-eminent part that Humber successes in cycle racing of all kinds had played in building up the firm's reputation and that of their machines. Humber's racing successes in the last quarter of the nineteenth century were so numerous that to list them all would be almost impossible and would make tedious reading. Let it suffice to say that such men as Fred Cooper, Keith-Falconer, Furnivall, G. Lacey Hillier, Herbert Synyer, H.E. Laurie and G.P. Mills in this country and Fernand Charron, H. Fournier and C. Terront abroad (to name but a few) were among the many who put the name of Humber among the leaders. On 'Ordinaries', tricycles and safety bicycles, Humber's were high in the lists of championships for many years. It was this reputation, gained by the heroes of the race tracks and the long-distance record bids, coupled with the unvarying quality of the machines themselves, no matter what the vagaries of the boardroom, that gave the make a reputation that survived long after the name had passed to Raleigh.

The firm was among several that produced the novel Pedersen 'Cantilever' frame design under licence in 1898. Licenced production ceased when Mikael Pedersen obtained his own factory at Dursley, Gloucestershire

The Motor Cycles

Humber motor cycles spanned a long period of almost continuous production, broken only from 1905 to 1909 by the pressing need to cope with increased car production, and later by the restrictions of the First World War. Apart from these short intermissions Humber's record of cycle, motor-cycle and car production under the same aegis must, by comparison with others – even Sunbeam – be one of the longest. Humber was early on the motor-cycle scene, *The Autocar* stated on 16 May 1896 that Humber had a display at the International Horseless Carriage Exhibition of 'motor cycles fitted with the Kane Pennington motors and two tandem safeties with the twin-cylinder motors boomed out at the rear.' Also from *The Autocar* of 6 June 1896 was a report which said that, 'The first practical motor cycle built in this country was completed last week when Humber & Co. finished a bicycle fitted with a Pennington two-horsepower motor made at their works in Coventry.'

The pioneering days of this enterprise were, it is true, of a somewhat faltering nature. Like a number of others who moved from the pedal-cycle field to that of powered machines, Humber relied heavily upon its cycle expertise. In many ways the strange recipes for powered machines that emanated from the Humber Works in these early days were no more strange than those of many of their rivals, and it is only in the light of later developments that one may nowadays regard them as unlikely contenders for success.

In 1896 H.J. Lawson paid Lèon Bollée £20,000 for the English manufacturing and patent rights and thus it came about that Humber made the first Lèon-Bollée *voiturette* built under licence in this country and followed this up with further small-scale production

A Lèon-Bollée-type Tricar of *c*. 1896. The first of these vehicles to be built in Britain was built by Humber.

of these odd little vehicles. The Humber Motors 1898 season catalogue offered the Lèon-Bollée-type machines as a 'Three-Wheel Motor Carriage (for three riders)'. This consisted of a two-seated forecar and what was basically a pedal cycle frame, handlebars and saddle-tube, with a pillar upon which the driver sat. It could be bought with a 2½ hp motor or with a two-cylinder motor and wheel steering at extra cost. Also listed were a Ladies' Motor Safety which was in fact a long-wheelbase lady's cycle frame of which the fore part was pure pedal cycle, but which had the motor mounted behind the saddle pillar. The catalogue described it as 'a long wheelbase machine fitted with a 1½ hp motor mounted on the frame which is directly connected to the driving wheel by chain drive.' However, the illustration clearly depicts belt drive. The specification continues: 'It is fitted with tube or electrical ignition, and in the latter case controlled by a small button on the handlebar.' A 28 in front and a 26 in driving wheel were fitted, with 1¾ in front and 2 in rear tyres. The only brake was a spoon brake on the front wheel, which, together with the odd weight distribution and no doubt a tendency to wag the tail, could hardly have contributed to the ladies' peace of mind. An even less likely contraption was the Combination Motor Tandem. Again, this was basically a pedal cycle design and could in fact be ridden as such in the event of motor breakdown, since a normal cycle rear wheel was provided which could be substituted for the powered one. The powered version had a 2½ hp motor driving on an axle which passed through the geared rear hub, thus enabling the motor unit to be disconnected, together with the fuel lines and carburettor. The machine had 28 in wheels back and front and

HUMBER MOTOR SOCIABLE.
(Coventry Production.)

hine has been designed to cater for those who prefer a two-seated vehicle, which enables the riders to sit side by side as in an
. It is practically the "Victoria" body, mounted on the same frame as described on page 6 with regard to the mechanis
s carefully hung on "C" springs, which eliminate the vibration from the road, and make it a very comfortable vehicle.

A Humber Motor Sociable of 1899. Based on the Lèon-Bollée design, the seating was side-by-side, hence the term 'Sociable'. It cost £170

double interconnected steering, but still only a front spoon brake for retardation. The only other powered machine offered was the Electrical Motor Tandem designed exclusively for pacing on cycle tracks. The catalogue proudly proclaimed 'It has attained a speed of forty miles an hour'.

Further developments offered in 1899 were the Motor Sociable version of the Lèon-Bollée, so called because the seating was side-by-side instead of the tandem arrangement of the other Lèon-Bollée-type machines. This machine weighed about 5½ cwt and cost £170. Of more obvious motor-cycle affinities, the firm also offered a De Dion-type tricycle with 1¾ hp air-cooled engine and a 2½ hp De Dion-type quadricycle.

The aftermath of the disastrous fire at the Coventry Works in 1896 and the equally disastrous crisis of confidence in the firm that resulted from the dismissal of Martin D. Rucker, the General Manager, and the whole Board of Directors following the

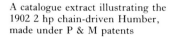
A catalogue extract illustrating the
1902 2 hp chain-driven Humber,
made under P & M patents

A catalogue extract illustrating the
1½ hp Minerva-type Humber of 1902

E.T. Hooley bankruptcy case, led to motor cycle development and
production being dropped for some years. By the time this was
resumed in 1902 what might be called the early gestation period of
motor cycle design was over and the lines of future development
could be more clearly determined. Certainly, Humber's new
offerings for the 1902 season were to set a very sound pattern for the
ensuing years.

Humber Ltd. had procured a licence to build a machine using
Phelon & Moore patents and turned out an excellent little 2 hp
chain-drive machine with the characteristic sloping engine mounting
in the front down tube. The transmission incorporated a spring
clutch to absorb jerk on the chains. The engine could be started on
the pedal gear and the bike could be pedalled as a normal cycle by
pegging the ratchet and pawl device. Frame parts were typical of
Humber's current pedal cycle practice, with rim brakes and, on the
Beeston version of the machine, the company's own patented
anti-vibration front fork. Again, strictly in accordance with Humber's cycle practice, the Beeston version was higher priced at £60,
while the Standard Special version cost £50. These were very

A close-up of the off side of the successful 1903 3 hp chain-drive model built under P & M licence

successful machines and laid the foundations of Humber's reputation in the motor cycle field.

In competition these machines did splendidly and notched up an enviable list of successes in this country and abroad. Humber Works riders J.F. Crundall (who was later to become the genial manager of the company's major London repair works at Canterbury Road, Kilburn) and Bert Yates were foremost in achieving these successes on road and track.

Also listed for 1902 was a 1½ hp belt-driven machine of Minerva-type which was listed at £55 for the Beeston model and £45 for the Standard Special. However, the chain-drive P & M machines proved much more popular, so for some years no belt-drive machines were offered.

The P & M-type motor cycles were offered in 1¾ hp and 2¾ hp form and fitted with a clutch in 1903. The 2¾ hp air-cooled engine was also fitted to a tricycle and the Olympia Tandem three-wheeler, which proved to be another popular introduction that was in its turn to be developed over the next few years. This improvement included water-cooling, hand starting, two-speed gears and coach-built fore-carriages. Lest the idea of carrying one's passenger out in front, where the risk from collision or accident was greatest, might seem a crude conception, it must be remembered that at this time the idea of a true sidecar (which became the accepted way to carry a passenger) was in its infancy, and many makes of three-wheeled forecars were available. Three-wheelers tended to become heavier, some embracing wheel steering instead of handlebars as the years went by, but by about 1907 such machines were on the wane.

"HUMBER"

What one could buy in 1903. The machine illustrated is the Beeston Humber Motor Bicycle

Variations on a three-wheel theme. This is the 1903 Humber Olympia Motor Tandem, and . . .

. . . this is the 2¾ hp Humber Motor Tricycle

Charming domesticity with a 1905
Humber Olympia Tricar De-Luxe,
the coachbuilt model with wheel-
steering. The photograph was taken
at Hamstead Mount, Handsworth
Wood, Staffordshire

In the last year of this phase of Humber motor-cycle production, 1905, the De Luxe version of the Olympia Tandem Forecar was offered with wheel steering as a Tricar, but motor cycles as such were discontinued owing to the imperative need to increase car production. There then followed a break until 1909, from when Humber motor cycles continued in production without interruption, other than that caused by the First World War, until the final demise of the motor cycle side of the business in 1930.

The 1909 re-birth offered one type of machine only, a 3½ hp single with air-cooling and the unusual feature of the exhaust silencer being incorporated in the front down tube of the frame. The engine was of 83 mm × 90 mm bore and stroke, there was handle starting, no pedalling gear, footboards, and a two-speed gear option. The front fork springing was also a little unusual. For some years, until the introduction of the big 6 hp water-cooled model in 1915, belt drive was to be the norm throughout the Humber range.

For 1910 the 3½ hp single underwent many detail changes. The most obvious to the casual observer was the abandonment of the

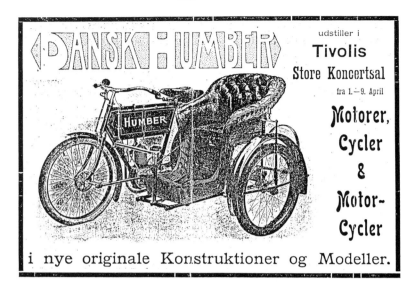

This illustration from a Danish trade journal shows the 5 hp Dansk-Humber of 1905, the last year of production

strange silencing arrangement. The front fork suspension was also altered and in general the machine was given a much neater appearance. It could be obtained with pedal gear as a single-speed machine, or with two-speed gear and free-engine clutch. A new model was also introduced in 1910 which became very popular and was continued with only minor alterations until phased out in 1914. This was a 2 hp lightweight single. Engine dimensions were 60 mm × 70 mm bore and stroke. It was a conventional little machine and was available in later seasons with free-engine hub at £4 extra over the basic price of £35 or with the option of an Armstrong three-speed hub gear at an extra 10 guineas. A Lady's model with dropped frame and gear-case for the pedalling gear was also available at £40, with the same optional extras at the same prices as the normal Light-weight.

The Works-backed sporting programme also re-emerged in 1910. Quite apart from the many competition events attended by Works and private riders, Humber Ltd. officially entered a team of five machines for the Tourist Trophy in the Isle of Man. These machines were all 3½ hp models, ridden by Yates, Wright, Crundall, Edmonds and Brown. The 2 hp and 3½ hp models were continued for 1911, the 3½ hp model being available as a single-speed machine with pedal gear or as a two-speeder by way of a Roc gear in the rear hub. A major success came when P.J. Evans won the Junior TT in the Isle of Man with his 2¾ hp V-twin model.

For 1912 the range consisted of the 2 hp Lightweight, the well-tried 3½ hp single and the 2¾ hp V-twin, the Tourist Trophy model. The 3½ hp was available with a choice of cane, wicker,

"HUMBER"

Near side of the 2 hp Humber Lightweight model introduced for the 1910 season. It was a popular little machine that continued in production until July 1914

Sam Wright, (No. 83), and Doug Brown, (No. 82) leave the line at the start of the 1910 Tourist Trophy in the Isle of Man. Other Humber riders, all on 3½ hp models, were J.F. Crundall, F.G. Edmonds and B. Yates

A 1911 3½ hp Humber with two-speed Roc gear is proudly exhibited by its owner, Bert Bladder, of Worcester

coach-built or commercial sidecars. The smart little TT model wore 'Come home to Daddy' handlebars, and could be bought with free-engine hub at £4 above the basic price or with three-speed hub gear at 10 guineas above the basic price of £42. The free-engine hub or three-speed option was also available on the Lightweight 2 hp models for the same additional cost.

The range was continued for 1913, a year in which F.G. Edmond, W.W. More, T. Knowles and Sam Wright all entered for the TT on the V-twin 2¾ hp models, giving Sam Wright sixth place, Tom Knowles twelfth and More twentieth. These race machines looked very neat with their round tanks and differed from the production models in having countershafts but not a countershaft gearbox. Chain drive from the engine ran to a plain countershaft from which belt drive continued the transmission to the rear wheel. By this

A catalogue shot of the 1914 2¾ hp Tourist Trophy model, so called in recognition of the success of the firm in the 1911 Junior TT with a similar model

Newly introduced for 1915 was this big passenger machine, the first Humber model to have a countershaft gearbox. It remained nominally in production right through the war, but few were made after 1916

means a reduction in gear ratio could be obtained between engine and countershaft, and a larger belt pulley on the rear wheel cut down belt slip. The Mk. VI Armstrong hub gears gave three speeds.

Just before the 1913 Motor Cycle Show Humber Ltd. turned out a most unusual machine which might be described as a three-cylinder opposed twin. It was a big 6 hp machine designed for sidecar work. The apparent anomaly of the cylinders was accounted for by the fact that it had the single (78 mm × 78 mm) cylinder facing forward and the twin (55 mm × 78 mm) facing to the rear. It had enclosed chain drive and three speeds in a countershaft gearbox. It appears that only one batch of these machines was made and records of these are very hard to come by. This model was described and illustrated in *The Motor Cycle* in September 1953, but any further details seem scarce.

The range was continued for 1914 with the addition of a water-cooled version of the 3½ hp single. The TT model featured dropped

An official Works photograph of the 4½ hp flat-twin in touring guise with a commodious Grindlay sidecar, which was endowed with better weather protection than some

bars rather than the staid touring style, resulting in a much improved appearance. The outbreak of war did not put an immediate stop to motor-cycle production – indeed, new models were introduced in 1915 and 1916. In the former year the 2 hp and 2¾ hp models were discontinued and a new 6 hp water-cooled flat-twin was introduced, and in 1916 a new air-cooled 3½ hp flat-twin of 68 mm × 68.75 mm came out. Very few models of these were produced and sadly, survivors are scarce. As Humber Ltd. became more seriously involved in the war effort and was particularly concerned with the production of aircraft and the development of W.O. Bentley's BR2 aero-engine, civilian production eventually came to a halt and no new motor cycles were turned out until 1919.

In 1920 the new offering for post-war buyers was again a flat-twin, of 4½ hp. It bore a superficial resemblance to the old 6 hp water-cooled model, but was the old 3½ hp air-cooled model with a slightly enlarged engine. The new model was designed for solo or sidecar work and was a refined and beautifully constructed machine. The engine was of 75 mm × 68 mm bore and stroke, giving a capacity of 600 cc. It had detachable valve seats, carburation was by Claudel-Hobson, transmission was all-chain via a three-speed

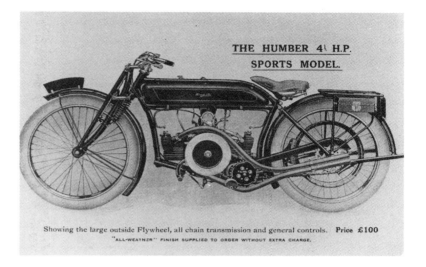

THE HUMBER 4 H.P.
SPORTS MODEL.

Showing the large outside Flywheel, all chain transmission and general controls. Price £100
"ALL-WEATHER" FINISH SUPPLIED TO ORDER WITHOUT EXTRA CHARGE.

Here the flat-twin is in Sports Model form and exhibits a nice line in exhaust pipes

countershaft gearbox and kick-starter, and, of course, magneto ignition. The touring model, with its wide handlebars, footboards and wide, heavily-valanced mudguards, was of staid appearance. Braking was a little primitive for a heavy machine of this type, being by dummy belt rim on the rear and stirrup on the front. The machine was very quiet and flexible, the company billing it as 'The Silent Humber'. Although the touring version had the old-fashioned expansion box slung low below the front down tube, the Sports Model had an exhaust system that involved some nice 'snake charming'. This was achieved by leading the pipe away high over the large outside flywheel, the pipe forming a graceful curve as it passed above the flywheel periphery, before dropping to run parallel for a short distance to its companion from the rear cylinder which had taken a downward curve to clear the clutch assembly, before the two pipes ran into an expansion box that ended in a short fishtail. The Sports Model's only other concessions to speed were footrests instead of boards and much slimmer, un-valanced, mudguards. It did retain the kick-starter, a point upon which the road-tester for *The Motor Cycle* commented favourably. He was less impressed with the braking. A range of sidecars was listed for this model and in later years a Lucas Dynamo Lighting Set was a catalogued option. Both models had quickly-detachable rear wheels.

In 1923 another new model was added to the range. This was a 2¾ hp single side-valve lightweight of 75 mm × 79 mm, giving 349 cc. This too was a very refined little machine which was available in touring, 'Six Days' (so called because of the excellent performance put up by these machines in the year of their introduction) and Sports versions. This model stayed in production after the

"HUMBER"

When the 4½ hp model was nearing the end of production the firm introduced this 2¾ hp (later called 3.49 hp) single, which remained the sole model, with variants, until motor-cycle production ceased

bigger flat-twin had been phased out. A sidecar option was available from 1925. Over the years, with this being Humber's only model remaining in production, a number of improvements came about. An overhead-valve engine was available for 1927 and, by 1928, almost the end of the road for Humber motor cycles, a very neat and attractive overhead-camshaft Sports model joined the stable. The Humber motor-cycle department still actively participated in competition after the First World War, the introduction of the 2¾ hp model sparking off a wave of trials riding by works Humber riders. Their success in the 1923 Six Days Trial has already been referred to. At the end of this very arduous event in which the Humber riders were L. Crisp, W.F. Newsome and the veteran Sam Wright, the side-valve 2¾ hp Humbers came away with the Team Prize and Certificate, a gold medal for each of the riders and best performance in the 350 cc Solo class. Justifiably proud of this success, Humber Ltd. published a lavishly-illustrated booklet recording the event in detail. Humber motor cycles enjoyed successes abroad, being awarded three silver cups, three medals and two first team places in the Austrian Alps Three Days Trial.

Unfortunately, not many 1920s riders remembered TT successes of the pre-1914 days and since there were no Works entries for the current events on the Isle of Man the overhead-camshaft Humber did not sell in any great numbers. Like all Humber products, it was a good-looking and beautifully-finished machine, but the writing was on the wall. The old guard who had actively championed the cause of motor-cycle competition were getting on in years and had less influence than once they may have done. Times had changed and the financial crash on Wall Street that heralded the 1930s made the

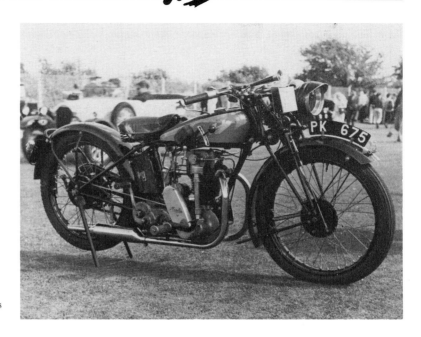

Top of the 3.49 hp range was this ohc model introduced in 1928. It was a very refined sporting mount

task of selling quality machines at profit that much harder. The increasing stake in Humber affairs being taken by Rootes, whose ideas did not embrace motor cycles, led to the motor-cycle flag being hauled down as 1930 closed.

As a postscript to this account of Humber motor cycles, it is worth mentioning a short-lived venture that sprang from the expansionist days of the cycle trade. Humber & Co. (Denmark) Ltd. was set up in 1897. As a cycle-maker it had enjoyed considerable success, but was phased out when the full realization of the disclosures at Hooley's bankruptcy were made public and it became essential to trim and rationalize Humber affairs very drastically under the newly-formed Humber Ltd. of 1900. Humber & Co. (Denmark) Ltd. became interested in powered machines through its support of cycle pacing for events and records. The company built some experimental machines in 1903 specifically for cycle pacing and the results were very encouraging. The firm decided to go into motor-cycle production in 1903/4. At this time the company was led by a director named Rothenborg who had V. Wennstrom as his Works Manager. Rothenborg engaged the services of Niels Petersen, the well-known constructor of Citus machines, who set about a production programme of touring, racing and pacing machines.

The three models of touring machines offered were all fitted with air-cooled single-cylinder engines of varying power. Smallest of the range was a 2¼ hp machine of 65 mm × 75 mm bore and stroke, followed by a 2¾ hp of 76 mm × 79 mm and a 5 hp model of

90 mm × 100 mm. The two smaller models had 28 in wheels shod with 2 in tyres, while the 5 hp had 2¼ in tyres. By contrast, the racing and pacing machines were twins, again with air-cooled engines. The smaller of the two was of 90 mm bore and 110 mm stroke and was said to give a maximum of 1,500 rpm. These pacing machines had very long handlebars and the rider sat right back over the rear wheel. One of these Dansk-Humbers had the distinction of winning the 100 km race at Ordrup track in 1903. In September 1904 Niels Petersen rode a longer and lower 5 hp racing machine with an engine weight of less than 50 kg when he took part in La Coupe Internationale du Motocycle Club de France. He used the trade name of 'Motor Jorgensen' in this event. The machine was a red-painted Dansk-Humber and the race was held on a circuit some 10 miles south-west of Paris. The start at 6.00 a.m. was heralded by much noise and celebration. Petersen was the favourite but much of the course was strewn with horse-shoe nails and punctures were prevalent, all entrants suffering much tyre trouble. On account of this, Petersen took over 54½ minutes to cover his second lap. Alas, on the third lap he suffered mechanical problems and had to retire. The tyre problems drastically reduced the field, and only three French and two Austrians riders finished the race. The winner was Demester.

For 1905 Dansk-Humber introduced a single-cylinder 4½ hp model of 90 mm bore and 110 mm stroke. This was a road racer model which, with its round, polished brass tank and white-painted finish had an elegantly aggressive look. In the Danish Motor Cycle Club's Relay and Baton Race on 5 June 1905 five Dansk-Humbers were entered, from which entry they gained first and second prizes. The smaller units for this season were V-twins of 66 mm bore and 70 mm stroke, rated at 3 hp. There was also a 'torpedo' version of this machine with a long wheelbase and handlebars almost as long as those on the cycle pacers, but the rider sat just forward of the rear wheel. These 3 hp twins were much more sedate-looking machines than the brass-tanked road racers.

At the AGM of the Dansk-Humber Co., held in October 1905, it was revealed that the cycle factory had made an annual profit of 8,072 Danish kroner, but the engine factory had made the staggering loss of 10,989 Danish kroner. This loss was the direct cause of the closure of the motor-cycle business. Unlike their British counterparts, whose motor-cycle production also ceased in 1905, the Dansk-Humbers were never resurrected. Niels Petersen, known as 'the engine doctor' on account of his skill in diagnosing and rectifying motor-cycle engine faults, went to serve the Danica concern.

The Dawn of the Motor Car

The early history of Humber cars has been described in the motoring press as 'surprisingly and maddeningly obscure'. Such indeed, has proved to be the case. Trying to throw light on this obscurity has not been helped by the fact that in the closing years of the 1890s the company underwent a severe crisis of confidence which blighted its esteem even in the cycling world. Much of this crisis was brought about by the policies and lifestyle of Martin D. Rucker and his unfortunate entanglements with personalities with whom he was connected. Reference was made in the discussion of Humber cycle history to the débâcle that occurred when one of Rucker's associates, E.T. Hooley, was bankrupted, bringing about Rucker's removal from office along with the entire Humber directorate. Fortunately, Hooley was not at this time concerned with the infant motor industry.

However, another of much the same ilk, H.J. Lawson, was thus concerned. 'He was probably no less scrupulous than many of the other remarkable characters who used other people's money to amass vast fortunes for themselves in the City of London at the turn of the nineteenth century. On the credit side, those who worked for him said that he was both fair and generous. He was certainly not a greedy man who loved money for its own sake.' This was the view of the late 'Bunty' Scott-Moncrieff in his classic book on veteran and Edwardian motor cars.

Lawson was no stranger to the cycling world, having already floated several companies and become a very rich man. He acquired the Daimler patent rights for England from F.R. Simms, having already formed the British Motor Syndicate, followed by the

THE HUMBER CAR.

| Net Cash Price | Standard ... | ... £275. |
| | Modele de Luxe ... | 300 Guineas. |

This catalogue illustration portrays the 1901 Humber with 4½ hp De-Dion engine. The car was unusual in having two forward and two reverse speeds

purchase of the English patent rights of every existing patent concerned with motor manufacture. Then, and almost certainly under Rucker's influence, he made a bad mistake. The British Motor Syndicate paid a plausible American from Chicago by the name of E.J. Pennington, £100,000 for his patents relating to motor cars. Many British firms, including Humber, took out licences from the British Motor Syndicate to build cars under Pennington patents. In 1896, Humber showed two tandem bicycles with Kane Pennington engines mounted astern of the rear wheel at the second Motor Exhibition at the Imperial Institute, London.

Unfortunately, many of Pennington's patents were impractical. Such vehicles as did see physical existence under Pennington's patents were weird and wonderful in the extreme, even allowing for the fact that at this period of motor-car history few in this country, with the possible exception of F.W. Lanchester, had any clearcut notion based on sound engineering principles of what they wanted to do in the automobile world. Humber itself seemed divided between a desire to produce vehicles of motor-cycle type and a wish to move into motor-car production. The authors have therefore decided to deal with those with a greater affinity to motor cycles, including tricars, in the chapter on motor cycles, and to treat as part of the motor history only those vehicles with four wheels. One of the 'maddening obscurities' was a motor car, described as a Humber, that was designed by Mr C.H. Shacklock, Manager of Humber's Wolverhampton cycle factory, in 1896. At the time of Mr Shacklock's death in 1934 *The Wolverhampton Express and Star* carried a photograph of this car with Mr Shacklock at the wheel. Alas, there were no particulars, and all trace of the original photograph has long since disappeared. The car appeared to be 'conventional' (if one may use such a term at this early stage of the motor industry) by comparison with other early Humber efforts but research has failed to yield any material on this particular vehicle. It is just possible that this may have been the car to which reference was made in the preamble to Humber's 1903 Motor Catalogue in which it is stated that 'as early as 1895 we experimented with an electric car, of which one of our engineers was joint inventor'. Obviously the design was not taken up, probably because Lawson's interests lay elsewhere. Reference is also made in the 1903 catalogue preamble to a 'large car of the belt-driven type [which] was made in 1899' which had the unusual feature of a mechanically-operated inlet as well as exhaust valves and forced lubrication.

By 1900 Humber had undergone another reorganization, becoming Humber Ltd., and at the same time breaking away from Lawson's influence. A programme of rationalization swept away all the old Hooley/Rucker-inspired factories and the Wolverhampton Works was also closed down. In this year Humber introduced a strange machine known as the M.D. Voiturette. As if front-wheel drive and rear-wheel steering were not an odd enough combination, this vehicle was started by the strange procedure of raising the steering wheel and giving it a sharp turn. This action operated a system of bevels, cross-shafts and chains to start the engine. The year 1900 also saw 3 hp, 3½ hp and 5 hp 'Phaeton' models produced.

The following year saw the first of a more conventional type of light car being turned out by Humber. In the introduction to the Humber Motors catalogue of 1901, is the remark, ' . . . In order to meet the present requirements we have found it necessary to concentrate our attention for the time being on the manufacture of light cars, which are at present so popular, and confine ourselves as far as the mechanism is concerned, to one standard pattern. . . .' This, at the very least, expresses a good intention after the haphazard and exploratory concoctions offered in the past. An implicit echo of the trials and tribulations of the complex patent rights battles of the late and unlamented Pennington and Lawson may be seen in the remark that, 'These cars are built under licence from the British Motor Traction Company, Limited, and embody all their latest improvements. Purchasers, therefore, need have no fear of being troubled with litigation for infringement, which at present is an important consideration, having in view the many cases which have recently been fought, and which are still pending.'

The cars in question were powered by 4½ hp water-cooled, single-cylinder De-Dion engines with De-Dion carburettor and coil and battery ignition. The transmission was by means of a live axle

In this view of the car the Humber-patented hinged radiator and the 'alligator' bonnet are shown to advantage. The accessibility thus provided was unusual though no doubt very welcome

Five up in a 1902 12 hp Humber. The expressions of driver and passengers suggest that motoring was a serious business

and shaft drive, with two forward and two reverse speeds. The brakes were on the transmission (pedal operated), with band brakes on the rear wheels operated by hand lever. The non-detachable wire wheels were of 28 in diameter shod with 3 in pneumatic tyres. Bodywork was a lightweight conventional tonneau. Springs were half-elliptics all round. A Humber patented feature was the hinged radiator which could be released from its normal upright position and lowered, while the 'alligator' bonnet could be raised by releasing a catch, thus rendering the entire engine compartment completely accessible. The Standard model of this car was priced at £275, the Modèle de Luxe at 300 guineas. The latter, to quote the catalogue again, was 'finished in the best possible style throughout, and, as a specimen of the kind of carriagework executed by an English carriage builder, is exceedingly handsome.' This was the first Humber car to make use of the single-spoke steering-wheel, a feature of all future models until 1910. Early in 1902 a larger-engined model of this type with a 9½ hp two-cylinder engine was also available.

A new 12 hp four-cylinder car designed by Louis Hervé Coatalen was produced in 1902. This proved to be a very successful design and was continued almost unaltered for 1903. Of 7 ft 0 in wheelbase and 4 ft 3 in track, the car had a patented tubular frame (Patent No.

The tubular chassis construction shows up very clearly in this view of a 1903 20 hp Humber. With an engine capacity of 5,347 cc and a wheelbase of 9 ft 6 in it was a powerful and commodious car

This style of body on the 20 hp Humber was the Roi de Belge. It cost 800 guineas with the honeycomb radiator shown here

6977 of 1902). Shaft drive and a live axle, four-speed gearbox, half-elliptic springing and battery and coil ignition were features of the specification, and Humber's patent hinged radiator was also fitted. Standard bodies were offered and so was the option of a body of the purchaser's choice, in which case the company was prepared to make an allowance of £40 in lieu of the standard body. An 8 hp two-cylinder car was also listed.

So successful was Coatalen's four-cylinder 'Twelve' that the following year, 1903, saw the introduction of a bigger version known as the 20 hp. Again this was a four-cylinder water-cooled car, of 4¼ in. bore and 5¾ in stroke. The entire specification was very similar to that of the '12 hp' with the exception that in the case of the 20 hp the front springing was transverse. The wheelbase was 9 ft 6 ins, the track remaining at 4 ft 3 in like the smaller car. The 20 hp was offered in standard tonneau-bodied form at 750 guineas, while the 'up-market' version with the new honeycomb radiator and a Roi-des-Belges body cost 800 guineas. The 'Twelve' cost 550 guineas and the allowance of £40 if a bespoke body was fitted in lieu of standard, was

The canopy and screens which adorn this Cornish-registered example of the 20 hp Humber would have added quite considerably to the overall cost

continued as in the previous year. The company designed and built a 9 hp three-cylinder car, one being entered in the Automobile Clubs Reliability Trial in September 1903. It suffered an accident the day before the Trials and did not take part. This model was not proceeded with.

The most significant production was that of the 5 hp single-cylinder Humberette, which first appeared in June, made both at Beeston and Coventry. This was the first Humber to be turned out in any numbers, 500 being produced in the first six months, of which 190 were from Beeston. The large number of surviving Humberettes pays tribute to their success and popularity, though their performance was necessarily modest. Enlarged versions were to appear before the design became obsolete, with the Humberette being dropped from the production programme for 1906. The 1904 specification reveals the following details: wheelbase 5 ft 3 ins; track 3 ft 6 in. The single-cylinder engine had a bore of 3⅝ in, was water-cooled and rated at 5.25 hp. The carburettor was a Longue-

A 1903 20 hp Humber. The original caption reads: 'We start for the Gordon Bennett course. This picture shows the car and its occupants at rest and touching the ground. This was not the normal condition, as when travelling the car seldom touched the ground, hence its name "The Aero Humber"'

mare and coil and battery ignition was used. There were two speeds forward and one reverse and, of course, shaft drive to a live axle. A separate lever was used to engage reverse gear; the handbrake lever was mounted further aft alongside the driver's seat. As was normal Humber practice, the footbrake operated on the transmission, the hand lever on band brakes on the rear wheels. The non-detachable wire wheels carried 28 in × 2½ in pneumatic tyres. The 6½ hp model, the Royal Humberette, and the other larger versions had artillery wheels instead of the wire pattern of the 5 hp car. Springing was half-elliptic front and rear. Standard colours were carmine with black mouldings and blue upholstery for the Beeston model, which also boasted bucket seats and side doors, and a governed engine with a pedal-applied accelerator. The Coventry model was without these refinements and could be had in dark green with black mouldings. Prices were 140 guineas for the Beeston version and 125 guineas for the Coventry model. The 6½ hp 'Royal' was priced at 160 guineas for the Beeston model and 150 guineas for the Coventry version. These cars had three forward speeds.

The company's catalogues included the motor cycles and forecars and the Humberettes with the pedal cycles, the larger cars featuring in the Motor Catalogue. Perhaps by this means the company hoped to win converts from pedal cyclists to its cheaper forms of motor transport, while at the same time encouraging those of greater means to seek a higher-priced motor car rather than a 'cheap' Humberette, forecar or motor cycle. The company seems to have been ambivalent about the use of prices in guineas or pounds (guineas having a snob appeal to the professional classes at this time), using both terms

The little single-cylinder 5 hp
Humberette of 1903 was a most
successful model which did more to
popularize the make than any of the
earlier offerings

indiscriminately, whether for describing the cheaper or the more
expensive of its motor vehicles.

The company was so pleased with the reception the Humberette
models had that it issued a lengthy publication entitled 'Letters of
Approbation, being a few testimonials commending the Humberette'. Some of these are from private individuals, care being taken
to include such titles as 'Doctor', 'Captain', 'Colonel' and so on,
while others are from Humber agents who enthuse about the
qualities of the cars and how well they are appreciated by their
clients. A complete novice wrote to remark that he had driven the car
home without a hitch, 321 miles, 'and never handled a motor car in
my life before', while a Col. G.J. Ross of Paignton remarked, 'The
car is easier to manage than a governess car and pony.' In general, it
was the hill-climbing abilities of the car and its reliability that clearly
impressed the owners, and economy of operation was another facet
that was often favourably commented upon.

Not surprisingly, the Humberettes appeared quite frequently in
the competitions of the time. It would be tedious to list these
appearances in full, so they may be sampled by reference to the

Automobile Club of Great Britain and Ireland (ACGBI) Small Car Trials of 1904 which took place between 29 August and 3 September, the event being based on Hereford. The total mileage involved was 620 and many hills were included. Humber Ltd. entered 6½ hp and 7½ hp versions of the Royal Humberettes as individual entries and not as a team. This being a trial confined to small cars and very strictly observed at all times, it afforded a fairer comparison than many of the merits or otherwise of the contestants. Humber Ltd. was awarded a Silver Medal for its cars' performances.

Edwardian
Optimism

Louis Hervé Coatalen, who had come to Humber in 1901 and was later to move to Hillman and then to Sunbeam, designed a small four-cylinder 8/10 hp model, for, despite the undoubted popularity and success of the Humberette in its various guises, the day of the under-powered, single-cylinder small car, however reliable, was obviously waning. At this time Coatalen was also responsible for a larger four-cylinder model, the 16/20 Beeston Humber, with cylinder dimensions of 95 mm × 125 mm. Despite a very conventional specification and no concessions to light weight this model proved to be surprisingly speedy. Coatalen, for whom motor competition and racing were to hold a life-long appeal, had an able and like-minded lieutenant in T.C. Pullinger who had been General Manager at Sunbeam and came to Humber in a similar capacity at Beeston. The 1905 16/20 model was, in fact, chosen to represent the company in the Tourist Trophy Race held in the Isle of Man.

For 1906, the Humberette range finally disappeared. The 8/10 hp introduced the previous year was enlarged to 10/12 hp and the 16/20 was introduced. Coatalen's 10/12 hp was highly successful, being turned out in such numbers that cars had to stand out in the streets for lack of space, even though several small works in Coventry were taken over to cope with the problem. At Beeston a very small number of six-cylinder cars of 30/40 hp were built. These totalled fourteen in all (chassis Nos. 3700–3713). Some doubt seems to exist as to their cylinder dimensions. P.N. Hasluck, writing in his *The Automobile,* Vol. 1, quotes 100 mm × 120 mm, rated at 40.8 hp. Humber itself quotes the bore as $4\frac{5}{16}$ in which equals 110 mm. Surprisingly, these cars had a round radiator much akin to the

This 1904 10/12 hp Beeston Humber has found its way to South Africa. Humbers were later exported widely, Australia and Brazil being popular choices

contemporary Delaunay-Belleville: other details were a wheelbase of 9 ft 11 in, a track of 4 ft 5 in, Krebs carburettor, dual ignition and cone clutch. The gearbox had four speeds and reverse. In terms of rated horsepower, these were the most powerful cars ever produced by the company.

Something of the success of Humber motor production at this period may be gauged by the company's profits which jumped from £6,537 in 1905 to £106,558 in 1906, a figure which was to expand to a staggering £154,537 in the following year. This was a profit figure that was not equalled until after 1932.

Further changes occurred in 1907. The 16/20 hp Beeston model was enlarged to 30 hp (110 mm × 130 mm) and was available in chassis form at £495. A variety of Humber-built bodies could be had on this chassis, ranging from the standard Roi-des-Belges tonneau at £525 to £675, for which sum it could be had with six-seater landaulette, limousine or berline bodies. The 10/12 hp continued unaltered, prices for this model ranging from £315 for the 'basic' four-seater (£270 in two-seater form) to £348 13s. for the four-seater equipped with hood and screen. A 'Doctor's Car' with leather hood, screen, horn and three lamps was available on the two-seater chassis for £300.

Newly introduced in 1907 was the 15 hp Coventry Humber, a four-cylinder car, with the cylinders having dimensions of 3¾ in × 4½ in. For some strange reason the company's catalogues quoted Beeston Humber dimensions in millimetres and Coventry-Humbers in inches at this period. The 'basic' Roi-des-Belges without hood or

8-10 h.p. FOUR-CYLINDER BEESTON HUMBER LIGHT CAR.

Price - - - - Net Cash. **300 Guineas.**

Complete Specification sent on application. *Free Trials arranged.*

"This is a very handsome two-seated vehicle, and is splendid value." *—The Motor.*

A catalogue shot of the 1905 8/10 hp Beeston Humber Light Car, already distinctive by reason of the prominent curved dash that marked the Beeston cars

screen cost £340 on this chassis and the most expensive option was a berline at £485. All the Humber bodies were beautifully built of first-class materials and very well finished. Standard colour for the 15 hp Coventry model was Humber green with black mouldings picked out in emerald green, while the 30 hp Beeston model offered standard colours of carmine picked out in black and lined in buff. For the landaulette and other closed body styles the standardized colour was dark green picked out in black, with red lining. Customers had the option of special colours at extra cost.

The Beeston models continued the policy of being 'up-market' in specification and price as compared with those made at Coventry. Whereas the 15 hp Coventry model for 1907 made do with three speeds operated by the quadrant change of old, the Beeston 30 hp car had four speeds and a gate change. All Humber models at this time continued to sport the distinctive feature of a single-spoke steering-wheel, from the centre of which sprouted the quadrant for the minor controls. The 10/12 hp model retained a tubular chassis – 'the Improved Tubular Frame' as the catalogue had it.

The 1907 catalogue itself reflected the growth and prosperity of the company's products, being a lavish affair of thirty-two pages as against the rather slender eight-page effort that had sufficed for 1906. The 1907 version, as well as giving full and well-illustrated specifications of all models, was filled out with several pages of press opinions and those of satisfied customers and users. Humber supplied a very ample tool kit in the price of each of its cars, but one must remember that as was usual at this period, a wide range of accessories, including lamps and much of the all-weather equipment, were extras to the basic catalogue price. For this reason

"HUMBER"

The 8/10 hp Coventry Humber of the same year has a swing-seat tonneau body. The rather unattractive radiator shape was short-lived, being altered the following year

The gardener stands by as the chauffeur-handyman pauses while attending to this 1906 10/12 hp Coventry Humber outside the motor house

several pages of the catalogue were occupied in listing a choice of such items together with their prices. Further catalogue pages were devoted to describing the Works and the main depots, as well as including a treatise on Humber cars in general terms.

Substantial changes were undertaken in 1908, not so much in the cars themselves as in the policies and administration of the company. By far the most costly and far-reaching of these changes was the decision to close down the old-established and frequently enlarged Beeston Works and to concentrate all car production at Coventry. For this purpose a new factory occupying some 22½ acres was opened in Folly Lane, now Humber Road, in March of that year. Again it was the irrepressible Walter Phillips, manager of Humber's Coventry Works, who coordinated the whole of this complicated reorganization and supervised the building of the new factory. This costly exercise also opened the directors' eyes to the need for more working capital by means of a new share issue, but progress in this direction was a little disappointing. *The Motor Trader* of 22 January 1908 recorded that of the 100,000 additional shares offered to shareholders in November 1907 at 30s. per share, only 39,174 were allocated, and consequently the directors were at that time (January 1908) offering 30,413 of the remaining shares at a premium of 5s. per share.

As for the new season's cars, these were substantially as for 1907 but with some significant additions. The 'old' 30 hp Beeston and 15 hp Coventry four-cylinder cars were joined by two newcomers, a 20 hp four-cylinder (105 mm × 130 mm) Beeston car and a Coventry-built 30 hp 'six' with cylinders 4 in × 4½ in bore and stroke. If one discounts the round-radiatored 30 hp 'six' of Beeston make, with only fourteen cars to the model's credit, the emergence of

The chauffeur is obviously proud of this gleaming 1906 16/20 hp Beeston model

the 1908 Coventry-built 30 hp 'six' was Humber's first 'production' six-cylinder car. The cylinders were cast in pairs, the engine had forced lubrication and dual ignition. With a wheelbase of 9 ft 10 in the car was fractionally shorter than the old Beeston 'six' and the longer bonnet necessitated by the six-cylinder engine meant that the bodywork was less commodious. Prices ranged from £450 for the open model without hood or screen to £600 for the six-seat limousine.

Beeston's 30 hp four-cylinder cars were somewhat confusingly classified. The 1907 20/30 hp of 110 mm bore was rated at 30 hp. These cars carried chassis numbers of 4001–4199. The next batch to be termed 30 hp in that year carried chassis numbers of 4200–4552, had a bore of 120 mm and were rated at 35.7 hp. For 1908 the 30 hp nomenclature was just as confusing, the cars with chassis numbers 4600–4850 had a bore of 105 mm and were rated at 27.3 hp. The final bunch for 1908 were of 120 mm bore, carried chassis numbers 4851–4997 and were rated at 35.7 hp, as had been the final batch for 1907. Make of that what you may! A catalogue footnote remarks that a self-starting arrangement could be fitted to the 30 hp Beeston models at an extra cost of £25. No mention is made of what form this took. It was either unpopular or unsuccessful, for no further mention is made of it on this or any other model until the advent of electric starters some years later.

The 20 hp Beeston model carried the catalogue subriquet of 'Light Tourist Trophy model' as some reflection of the participation of the successful Beeston Humbers in the 1907 event, though in fact the 'Light 20 hp' car in the race was by no means of standard specification. Unlike the larger 30 hp Beeston model, the four

A 30 hp Beeston Humber takes three Cornish gentlemen and their dog out into the countryside

cylinders of the new 20 hp were cast separately. Amusingly, one notes in the catalogue specification that 'this engine may be run up to 2,000 rpm' in bold print. Prices ranged from £425 for the four-seat tonneau to £595 for the six-seat landaulette or limousine. (The notion of Lady X alighting from her 'Tourist Trophy' model landaulette or limousine seems, to say the least, to be stretching the bounds of credulity.)

Offered on the 10/12 hp Coventry car were two styles of Motor Cab, one a two-seater, the other a four-seater. This terminology is not as straightforward as it would appear at first sight, for the number of seats in this case indicates the number of *passenger* seats and, paradoxically, the four-seater Motor Cab was of shorter wheelbase than the two-seater version at 7 ft 1 in and 8 ft 0 in respectively. This was achieved by adapting the four-seater version so that the driver sat aloft above the engine and bonnet, in effect giving forward control. This version was given more power by

A 1907 15 hp Coventry Humber
receives a little loving care from the
family. Note the characteristic
Humber oil can being put to good use

increasing the bore by a quarter of one inch to cope with the
increased weight. Both the two- and four-seater Motor Cabs
complied with Scotland Yard's regulations for Hackney Carriages.
At £300 for the two-seater Motor Cab and £350 for the four-seat
version these were the most expensive of the 10/12 hp range.

Despite this attractive range of Beeston and Coventry cars, 1908
proved to be a poor trading year. This, coupled with the expensive
decision to close the Beeston factory and concentrate car production
at Coventry, and the consequent building of the new factory, played
havoc with the company's profits. At the directors' meeting, Edward
Powell, the Managing Director, had the unpleasant task of
explaining that in strong contrast to the reports of the previous few
years he had to announce a loss of £23,000, all of which had been
incurred in the motor department at Coventry. Trade had fallen off
badly and the company found itself in the position of having an
enormous number of cars coming through the Works that it knew it
would be difficult to dispose of during the season. As a result of this

Walter Phillips, who, as Works Manager of the Humber Coventry Works from 1892 to 1910, gave such sterling service, is seen here at the wheel of a 1908 10/12 hp four-seater

situation the company had had to allow its agents larger discounts and to sell cars at less favourable terms than it had anticipated at the beginning of the year. The Beeston Works had made a very reduced profit and the cycle departments at Beeston and Coventry had also made reduced profits.

Long and somewhat acrimonious discussions followed and Earl Russell moved an amendment that consideration of the report and accounts be adjourned and that an independent committee be appointed to look into the causes leading to the fall off in the company's profits, to ascertain the present position, to consider proposals for the reconstruction of the company and to report its findings to an adjourned meeting. In the event, all but one of the company's directors resigned.

As for the cars themselves in the 1909 programme, these comprised the 30 hp six-cylinder model, the 20 hp four-cylinder and the 12 hp four-cylinder of old, but with two newcomers added to the range. These were the 8 hp two-cylinder and a 16 hp four-cylinder model. The small 8 hp, with cylinders of 90 mm × 120 mm, was made only in two-seater form at £195. However, it shared with the other new model of the season the use as standard of Humber's own design of detachable wheel. This was a neat centre-locking device in which the drive was taken by six studs on the inner face of the wheel hub, which engaged in corresponding holes in the main hub on the stub axle. These Humber detachable wheels were available in wooden 'artillery' form or as wire wheels. The company's catalogue claimed that a wheel of this type could be changed in three minutes.

"HUMBER"

An unusual commercial van body graces this 1908 20 hp Beeston Humber which was adapted from the car chassis by lengthening and strengthening to suit. It is fitted with solid tyres

These wheels could be fitted to other models of the range on request at extra cost, and the company also offered to convert its 1908 10/12 hp, 20 hp Beeston models and 30 hp six-cylinder models at the request of owners, at a charge of £23 to £27 depending on the wheel and tyre sizes.

The new 16 hp car was a four-cylinder model with the cylinders cast separately, with dimensions of 100 mm × 130 mm. It had dual ignition as standard and a four-speed gearbox with gate change. Prices ranged from £385 for the standard tonneau to £555 for the six-seated D-front landaulette. Standard colours were Humber carmine, blue or green, with dark green picked out in black, 'suitably lined' for the closed bodies. The 12 hp model continued almost unchanged but with some new body options. One of these was the Doctor's landaulette, available at £330 to £342 10s. with extension and screen. It was intended, of course, that the doctor would employ a chauffeur. This model was equipped with, to quote the catalogue, 'polished walnut cabinet with drawers fixed to front . . . upholstered in very best manner with drab corded cloth and lace . . . adjustable electric lamp and speaking tube . . . space under seat for handbag.' Just the Humber for Harley Street. In a different social stratum there was offered new that year, the 12 hp Traveller's Car, priced at £350. Of this the catalogue remarked, ' . . . interior fitted with polished roof and side panels, and on the right side five polished shelves, four of which are easily adjusted by means of brass slides to suit any size package. A seat is provided inside the car and another at the side of the driver, making it a most complete car for business purposes.' A normal four-seater Motor Cab was offered but the two-seat version was withdrawn.

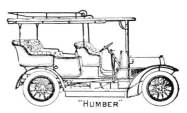

"HUMBER"

This 1909 12 hp Humber was first registered as AB 1151 on 11 March 1909. It was finished in Humber carmine. A 1909 3½ hp Humber motor cycle stands behind it

So, as 1909 drew to a close, Humber Ltd. was making a careful re-appraisal of its policy in the earnest hope that that policy would allow the solid worth of its products to find satisfied customers, as well as doing everything in its power to offset the misfortunes of the year just ending.

Edwardian Caution

The catalogued Humber range for 1910 revealed little apparent change from that of the previous year, comprising the two-cylinder 8 hp (which under the new RAC rating came out at 9.8 hp), the 12 hp, which, with an increase in stroke, of 5 mm to a new figure of 100 mm, was rated at 20.8 hp, the bore dimension remaining unchanged, and the 16 hp, rated at 24.79 hp. The new season's catalogue included graphs showing the speed and gear ratios of each model, together with details of the new tax likely to be levied under the Budget proposals. The 16 hp now had its cylinders cast in pairs, bringing it into line with the rest of the range. Humber's detachable wheels, featured at length, were now standard throughout the range, as was the option of the wire wheels in lieu of wood. Certainly, these wire wheels had been thoroughly tested under the most rigorous conditions before becoming standardized throughout the range, for Humbers so fitted had performed very successfully in many long-distance reliability trials for which the company had officially entered.

New body styles on the 12 hp in its revised form included a landaulette and a limousine and what was amusingly termed a 'Racing Type two-seater' with the quickly detachable wire wheels as standard. These apart, the only concession to a 'racing type' seems to have been the provision of a less angular body with a bolster petrol tank to the rear of the two seats. It was priced at £285, the same as the standard bodied four-seater. However, all models of the 12 hp were increased in price as from 1 May 1910 and again on 15 August 1910 'owing to increased cost of production'. Prices for the 16 hp car were also up on those for the previous year, ranging from £410 to

"HUMBER"

A Humber catalogue photograph that set out to demonstrate the ease and speed with which the newly-introduced Humber quick-detachable wire wheels could be changed, even by the ladies. Humber Ltd. claimed that a wheel could be changed in three minutes

£590. However, these can only be taken as approximate as so many options of type of windscreen, finish and so on were available with consequent variations in the overall price.

For 1911 there appeared two new models, the first being the 10/14 hp (RAC rated at 14.3 hp), a four-cylinder car of 76 mm × 110 mm bore and stroke. This model was catalogued only as a two-seater with Humber's detachable wire wheels at £295. It could be had in chassis form for £270. A four-speed gearbox was fitted, so that for the first time in the company's history all its range was four-cylindered with four-speed gearboxes. As in 1910, the catalogue included graphs showing the speeds on gears. Perhaps a swing in fashion dictated that in this year the wire wheel version of the quick-detachable wheels was standard wear, the artillery type available 'to order'. Certainly the standardization of the wire wheels did much to offset the rather heavy-bodied appearance of most of the cars, particularly those with closed coachwork. The old 12 hp was now termed the 12/20 hp and the old 16 hp became the 16/24 hp.

The other new introduction of the 1911 season was the largest of the range, at 28 hp. (RAC rated at 27.3 hp). This was a lusty four-cylinder car of 105 mm × 140 mm, the cylinders cast in pairs. It was available in two wheelbase lengths, 9 ft 10 in or 10 ft 10½ in, and was obviously intended to carry commodious and well-appointed formal bodywork rather than open styles, though a two-seater without extras was catalogued at £465 and also a double

This splendid 1910 16 hp model is still active and cherished in Norway, to which country it was exported when new

phaeton at £490. The more imposing six-seater closed body styles were mounted on the longer of the two wheelbase options.

It was in this year that the overall appearance of all models in the Humber range first exhibited a close and general similarity, each smaller model being almost identically a scaled-down version of a larger one, a characteristic that was to remain evident into the 1930s, so that at a casual glance it was not easy to distinguish one model from another.

The year 1912 found new models listed and also some surprising specification details that might almost be said to be retrogressive. One such was a reversion to three speeds in the smallest of the new models (the 11 hp) and Humber-pattern, wire *non-detachable* wheels also on this model. To be fair, the detachable pattern could be had at extra cost. The 11 hp did, however, break new ground as far as Humber was concerned by being its first four-cylinder monobloc engine.

The 14 hp model with cylinder dimensions of 78 mm × 110 mm had also reverted to a three-speed gearbox. Now rated at 15.1 hp this model was available with two- or four-seater open body or what the catalogue was pleased to term 'coupé limousine' or 'coupé land-aulette' bodies. A later generation would have termed these body styles as 'fixed head' or 'drophead' coupés. At £395 for either coupé this was the most expensive on the 14 hp chassis, but the same body styles could be had on the 11 hp for £370. One might be forgiven for becoming somewhat confused over the identities of the 12–20 hp and the 20 hp models. The former, with bore and stroke of 90 mm ×

This version of the same model wears the quick-detachable wire wheels which do much to lighten the overall appearance

100 mm, the four cylinders cast in pairs, was only available in open two- or four-seater forms; the latter, with the same 90 mm bore but the stroke increased to 120 mm and still RAC rated at 20.1 hp, was offered with a much more extensive choice of body styles and, like the larger 28 hp, on the long or short wheelbase options. Prices for the 20 hp model ranged from £370 for the simplest two-seater to £650 for the Pullman limousine on the long chassis. This style, with its short bonnet and immense length of lofty closed bodywork which included windows that would not have been out of place along the corridor side of a railway carriage, looked ideally suited to the function of a mourners' car at a high-class funeral. It was also available on the longer of the two wheelbases on the 28 hp car at £755. Another unusual feature, for Humbers, was worm final drive on the 20 hp car, presumably introduced in the interests of silence as compared with bevel drive. The catalogue coyly states, ' . . . the car has a good reserve of power and with worm drive is very silent.'

This 1911 12/20 hp Humber was photographed in Rio de Janeiro, Brazil, in 1912, where it was in use as a taxi. The early taxi-meter is of interest

Theodore James Biggs had two spells of employment with Humber Ltd. He had first come to Humber late in 1906 and had been much concerned while at Beeston with the three Beeston-built overhead-camshaft TT racers of 1908. Closely associated while at Beeston with T.C. Pullinger, Biggs had gone with Pullinger at the latter's invitation to Arrol-Johnston on 10 April 1909. Biggs' association with the Scottish firm was short but productive. Nevertheless, he returned to the Humber fold, now entirely centred on Coventry, on 15 April 1912. It was Biggs who was largely responsible for the design of the new series of 11 hp and 14 hp Humbers that were catalogued from 1912 to 1914, and the 10 hp introduced for 1914.

The first tangible results of Biggs' return to the Humber fold became evident in 1913. In that year the catalogued 11 hp car differed little in outward appearance from its counterpart of the previous year. What Biggs did with this model was to remove the anomalies and update the specification. The four-cylinder monobloc engine was sound enough, but for 1913 the bore and stroke was 69 mm × 130 mm. A longer wheelbase of 8 ft 11 in was used for the four-seater, and the old 1912 length of 8 ft 4 in was used only on the two-seater cars, though the track in both cases was widened from 4 ft 2 in to 4 ft 7 in. A four-speed gearbox was now standard on this model and the old anachronism of the non-detachable wheels was swept away, the normal Humber wire, quick-detachable wheels being shod with 810 mm × 90 mm tyres. Standard finish was Humber green, stone grey to order, with black chassis and wheels. Other colours could be had at extra cost. The car was RAC rated at

The Humberette name reappeared in 1913 in the form of this air-cooled V-twin cyclecar. It was a popular and successful model. This example wears Worcester City Council Trade Plates FKC–1

For 1914 a water-cooled option was available on the Humberette and in 1915 the air-cooled version was no longer listed

11.9 hp and sold at £295 for the two-seater or £310 for the four-seater, fully equipped.

The new 14 hp was not the same as the old 14 hp of 1912. (Another example of the confusion in Humbers' nomenclature at this period.) Like the new 11 hp, this new 14 hp now had a monobloc four-cylinder engine of 75 mm × 130 mm rated at 13.9 hp. Wheelbase was 9 ft 2 in and track 4 ft 7 in. A four-speed gearbox was fitted with different ratios for the two- and four-seater cars. Like the new 11 hp, this 14 hp had electric side and tail lights, but in the case of the 14 hp model only, a No. 5 Rotax-Leitner

The 10 hp Humber was a thoroughly up-to-date, well-equipped small car introduced for the 1914 season. The buyer of this example evidently mistrusted the electric lighting system that was available on this model

dynamo lighting set could be had for an extra £18, including fitting. The 20 hp and 28 hp models continued with only detail changes, including electric side and tail lamps and the full dynamo lighting option.

At the bottom of the range, the Humberette name made a reappearance, this time as a cyclecar of rather more refined aspect than most of the breed. Cyclecars had caught the public's fancy about 1912 and mushroomed in many and varied forms, and usually rather crude. The new Humberette was a V-twin with air-cooled engine of motor cycle type, and cylinders of 84 mm × 90 mm bore and stroke. Like its earlier namesakes, the chassis was tubular but the elementary and often troublesome belt or chain drive of many of its cyclecar contemporaries was firmly eschewed; instead it had a live axle and bevel gear. The steering was by rack and pinion, suspension was by a transverse spring at the front and ¼-elliptics at the rear. A three-speed and reverse gearbox was fitted for which the old-fashioned quadrant change was deemed good enough. It was indeed a tiny car with a wheelbase of only 7 ft 5 in and a track of 3 ft. 6 in. Wheels were non-detachable wire shod with 650 mm × 65 mm tyres. In two-seater form (there were no other body options) it sold for £125 complete with screen, hood, horn and three lights. It proved to be quite a lively performer and its standard of finish was superior to that of most of the cyclecar breed. It thus became a popular model. Sam Wright was frequently to be seen at the wheel of a Works-entered Humberette in many of the trials of the period and he gave convincing proof of the little car's stamina and performance.

The Motor of 18 November 1913 remarked that since Humbers' 1907 profit figure of £154,000 'maintenance and depreciation have

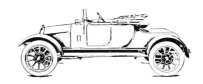

The 1914 14 hp, of which this is a surviving example, was developed into the post-war 15.9 hp

absorbed the trading profits, the expenditure of an abortive aeroplane department having been nearly £13,000. However, the corner appears to have been turned . . . ', going on to quote 'last year's net profits were £50,091 2s. 6d.' 'Abortive' the aeroplane department may have been, but the boldness and vision of Mr Ballin Hinde, a Humber director and keen aeronaut, and those he was able to persuade to his cause, must surely have paid off in the upheaval that war was to bring in 1914.

In so many senses 1914 was a watershed. Cataclysmic events were to occur before its close but long before that Humber Ltd. engaged in a costly and uncharacteristic venture in the building of a team of special cars for the newly-resurrected Tourist Trophy in the Isle of Man. Perhaps someone in Humber's high places couldn't resist the 'glamour' of sending cars to those old races in which the company had taken part so steadfastly, if not with much success. Humber had been represented in every one of the Tourist Trophy races in the Isle of Man.

As for the 1914 production cars, there was only one real newcomer among them in the shape of a 10 hp model which was, as events turned out, to be the basis of a range that continued until 1927. The new 'Ten' featured a four-cylinder monobloc sidevalve engine with the surprisingly 'modern' inclusion of a detachable head and unit construction of engine and gearbox. Wheelbase was 8 ft 9½ in and track 4 ft 7 in and the car was available in open two-and four-seater form. Offered at first with electric side and tail lights but acetylene headlights (an option that remained but was seldom taken), it was soon to be offered with full dynamo lighting and CAV electric

The 1914 11 hp retained the Humber wire wheels, whereas the newly-introduced 10 hp and 14 hp models were fitted with steel artillery wheels, without the benefit of the Humber-patented, quick-detachable device

starting at an increased price. The CAV starting system was similar to that on its bigger brother, the 14 hp, this latter having these refinements from the beginning of the 1914 season. With the full electrics the price of the 'Ten' rose from £235 to £255 in two-seater form, and from £250 to £270 for the four-seater. Thus equipped the little 'Ten' was thoroughly well-found, an up-to-date small car embodying a standard of finish, comfort and completeness that was well above the average for small cars of its time. This model and the 14 hp wore detachable steel artillery wheels (bolt-on), whereas the 11 hp, the 20 hp and the 28 hp continued to make use of Humber detachable wire wheels so familiar over the previous few seasons.

A new option on the successful little Humberette was now available in the form of a water-cooled version at £135, complete with screen, hood, horn and three lamps and a set of tools, £15 more than the air-cooled model similarly equipped. Standard colours were brown for the 'Ten' and stone grey (green to order) on the 11 hp and 14 hp cars, whereas the 20 hp and 28 hp cars retained the standard and optional colour choices of the previous season. No closed models were offered on the 'Ten' or the 11 hp, but the 14 hp offered a

This commercial van body has been adapted to a 1915 11 hp tourer, thereby enjoying full electric lighting and starting which the catalogued vans on this chassis lacked

four-seater landaulette at £520 and a coupé-landaulette at £480. The most expensive of the entire range was the 28 hp six-seater cabriolet at £650.

The outbreak of war did not immediately bring car production to a halt, and a full catalogue was produced for 1915, only to reveal a number of changes. The two larger models were discontinued and production was centred on the 10 hp, 11 hp and 14 hp. The air-cooled version of the Humberette was also dropped. Prices were increased and some 'warlike' options introduced in the form of delivery vans on the 10 and 11 hp chassis and an ambulance on the 'Fourteen'. Also in 1915, the year in which civilian production virtually stopped, the main range of Humber cars were all offered with full dynamo lighting and electric starting. The Humberette and the 'commercial bodied' variants of the larger models did not include these refinements. The 'Ten' and the 'Fourteen' were to continue, albeit mothballed for the present, to emerge again when hostilities ended, and with greater or lesser change to form the backbone of the initial post-war programme. That these models, which owed much to T.J. Biggs' hand, were really sound is borne out by the fact that with modifications of a comparatively minor nature they both lasted until 1927. It must be admitted, though, that a firm of less conservative outlook might well have made more radical changes to its programme at a slightly earlier stage. The man responsible for the design of the 'Ten' and 'Fourteen', however, had again left Humber's employ on 16 November 1914 to take up a post with F.E. Baker Ltd., Precision Engines, Birmingham.

On Road and Track

Humber cars have for so long epitomized the touring car of quality that it is difficult to come to terms with the fact that at one period in the company's history they played an active part in motoring competition. If one is to attempt to place such activities in perspective when viewed against the whole background of the company and its products over the period with which this book is concerned, some consideration must be given to the circumstances that influenced, or may have influenced, both its active participation in motor competition and its withdrawal in later years.

First, it must not be forgotten that in its pre-motor-cycling heyday the firm had been in the van of competition events and it is not unreasonable to suppose that the many ex-racing cyclists who became middle or senior staff by the time motors were establishing the Humber name, may still have been imbued with something of the competitive spirit. Secondly, competitive events in the early years of motoring served a useful double purpose in that they tested the product under the most strenuous conditions and any successes gained in such competitions were a valuable form of advertisement. For this reason, probably the majority of motor manufacturers, even those that were only involved in the industry in a small way, took part in motor competition to some degree. In such cases the competing cars were most often the standard products of the company or were largely standard with only minor modifications. Only those makers with substantial financial resources could afford to build highly specialized cars that differed radically from their standard products in order to compete in the *grands epreuves* of Continental motor racing. It must also be remembered that Britain's legislation put her at a distinct disadvantage in this respect, it being impossible to hold such events in this country.

A third important factor lay in the personalities of those in the higher ranks of the company, particularly that of the designer or chief engineer. A strong personality in such an office, and one who believed in competition as a spur to design and success, with its attendant publicity as a boost to sales, could do much to persuade a possibly disinterested board to allow the financial expenditure and the use of manpower to set up a progressive competitions department and to sanction Works support for the cars entered in various events.

Lastly, there are the 'outside' factors to take into account, such as the restrictions or formulæ that governed the entries to such events. Changes in these factors were largely unforeseeable and could therefore result in heavy expenditure, brought about by the need to build cars to different or changing formulæ or race regulations. These might take the form of restrictions of cylinder bore, or more rarely, stroke, of chassis dimensions, of overall weight, petrol consumption over the duration of the race (which in turn led to the most careful consideration of gear ratios, carburation, the nature of the course itself and the number of laps to be covered) and so on.

Humber's approach to the competitive side of motoring was typically cautious. Only twice in the years that led up to the First World War did the company ever turn out cars for competitive events that differed radically from its normal products. It is ironic that both these departures from the customary caution were totally unrewarding in terms of success. Yet these same departures, puzzling though they are, are of fascinating interest in themselves, if only for the number of unanswered questions they raise. On both occasions they involved the building of Humber racing cars for specific reasons; also no attempt seems to have been made to follow up and develop the interesting designs that evolved. Indeed, the company seems to have been keen to wash its hands of the matter as quickly as possible!

From the foregoing it will be seen that Humber's successes in the field of motor competition came from its use of standard, or largely standard, cars in the sort of events in which quality of the product, reliability, plus, of course, skilful driving, could bring success. In the years up to 1914 a handful of Works drivers and many more private owners kept the Humber name well to the fore with regard to places and awards in the many events that were held up and down the country and even overseas. Broadly speaking, these events could be divided into two types, the long-distance reliability trial and the short distance sprint or hill-climb.

It will come as no surprise to students of motor sport in the early years that Humber's first rather tentative entry came during the time

This 7½ hp Royal Humberette was one of the firm's entries in the ACGBI Small Car Trials based in Hereford in 1904. It is seen here in The High Street, Hereford

that Louis Hervé Coatalen was in charge of Humber design at Coventry. His appointment to Humber Ltd. at Coventry was his first important post in this country. Two of his first design for Humber, the 12 hp four-cylinder model, were entered for the ACGBI's 650-mile Reliability Trial in 1902. One of these cars was driven by H. Belcher who, like so many senior men at Humber at the time, was an ex-racing cyclist who had become General Manager of the Beeston Works in 1895. Although the cars achieved no marked success in the Trial, the new 20 hp of 1903 made an impressive debut at the 'Irish Fortnight' that followed the Gordon Bennett Trophy Race of that year. The 'Irish Fortnight' involved both speed trials and hill-climbs in which J.W. Cross's 20 hp Humber did remarkably well.

On the mainland in 1904 Belcher enjoyed a number of successes with a 25 hp Humber, but he resigned in the same year and was succeeded by T.C. Pullinger who had come from Sunbeam. Coatalen was still at Coventry and no doubt found that Pullinger's firm belief in the value of competition success as a means of promoting public interest, and therefore sales, was much in accord with his own opinions. It is significant that it was during the period when Pullinger was with Humber Ltd., even after Coatalen's subsequent move to Hillman (where his stay was but a short one prior to his next move to Sunbeam), that a much more active competition policy was embarked upon and that there occurred the first of the two untypical and radical departures from normal Humber design for, it appears, purely competition purposes.

Pullinger himself moved from Humber to Arrol-Johnston in 1909 (by which time Coatalen had left Hillman and was installed with Sunbeam at Wolverhampton), taking with him, among others, Theodore James Biggs. Biggs, like so many men in the motor trade at this time, was an ex-racing cyclist, a draughtsman/designer who had earlier spent three periods with Raleigh interspersed with ventures into motor manufacture. He then came to Humber at Beeston late in 1906. There he came into close contact with Pullinger. Thus we have Pullinger and Biggs both at Humber Ltd. (Beeston), at a period when Humbers were most active in competition. This was followed by a spell when Humber was less active in this field, after Pullinger and Biggs moved on to Arrol-Johnston.

To see the 1904–9 Pullinger period at Humber in perspective one must glance at what happened in Scotland at Arrol-Johnston in the next few years when Pullinger and Biggs were there. This period, 1909–12, saw a sudden upsurge of interest in competition on the part of Arrol-Johnston which entered cars for the 1911 Coupe des Voiturettes and again for the Coupe de l'Auto in 1912, as well as appearing in a number of sprint events in this country and indulging in record-breaking at Brooklands. Such activities on the part of the Scottish firm were as much out of character as they had been at Humber, for the Arrol-Johnston production cars were of an even more staid mien than were the production Humbers, despite the 'glamour' of Arrol-Johnston having won the very first Isle of Man Tourist Trophy in 1905 with the J.S. Napier-designed two-cylinder car. There are other links that will be explored more closely later.

Coatalen's new basis for his Humbers' competition successes in 1905 was the range of 8/10 hp, 10/12 hp and, particularly, 16/20 hp cars and the introduction of a race for cars of basically touring specification in the form of the Isle of Man Tourist Trophy Races initiated in 1905. This was a splendid opportunity for him to put his ideas into practice. Two 16/20 hp cars destined for the TT were given preliminary competitive airings at sundry sprint events in this country. For the great race itself they were driven by G.H. Cooper and Jimmy Reid, the cars being entered by Pullinger on behalf of the company. They were heavy cars, only just coming within the upper weight limit permissible under the regulations, and neither was very successful.

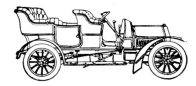

For the 1906 TT, however, Pullinger himself drove a 16/20 hp Beeston Humber to which some attention to paring excess weight

C.H. Cooper in the unique chain-driven 60 hp Beeston Humber at the *Graphic* Trophy Race held over a 4½-mile course in the Isle of Man after the TT race in 1906. His time was 5 minutes 15 seconds

had been given, while Coatalen drove the Coventry Humber contestant, a 20 hp car of marginally smaller cubic capacity but, alas!, extravagantly greater weight, scaling no less than 1,903 lb when the minimum permissible was 1,275 lb. The race regulations also called for a minimum of 25 mpg overall. It is worth including an amusing extract from the island's press, taken from an interview with Coatalen who had F. Howarth as his mechanic in the 20 hp Coventry car.

Mr Coatalen, who designed and drove the 16–20 hp Coventry Humber, which was built for the Circuit Europèen, was humorous touching his prospects. 'When you see me do the circuit in 52 minutes you can say to yourself, "He is not doing the consumption, the bounder," for I must crawl on top gear all the way round to Ramsey to do it; but . . .' (and here his accent has traces of the Frenchman) 'ven I get on to ze level – then to me is the space! Zey come to me and zey say, "I can do the course in 55 minutes and haf half a gallon left." I tell zem, "Oh, zat is nothing. I do him in 45 minute." I haf a gallon and a half left because I freeveel all round ze course and up over Snaefell too. Eef there is a smash I tink certainly some of zem will go downwards. But I am allright. I haf a very good boy for my mechanician. He never swear, but always go to church on Sunday; so I say to him, "If we haf a smash I shall hang on to you – you must introduce me!".'

The two Humbers performed well and reliably, Pullinger having a trouble-free race and finishing in fifth place, Coatalen coming in in sixth place, thus allowing Humber to be the only 'make' team to finish complete. Their overall speeds were 32.6 and 32.1 mph respectively. The winning Rolls-Royce averaged 39.3 mph.

For the following year the regulations were changed and the TT entries were divided into 'Heavy' and 'Light' categories and Humber competed in both. Two cars were entered in each category. W.G. Tuck (a Works driver of whom much more will be heard) drove a 16/20 hp Coventry Humber, Jimmy Reid, a 16/20 hp Beeston Humber of slightly smaller overall capacity in the 'Light' race, while G.H. Cooper and G.P. Mills (the same Mills who had earned for Humber so many cycling records as to become something of a legend in the days before the motor car) drove 30 hp Beeston Humbers in the 'Heavy' category, in which the cars were encumbered with a stout vertical shield intended to produce the drag equivalent to the frontal area of a normal closed car.

Weather conditions for the event were of the inclemency that only the Isle of Man can, and often does, provide on occasions. In the 'Light' category Reid came in second place behind the winning Rover, these cars being the only cars out of the twenty-two starters to finish. To cap Humber's delight the 'Heavy' event was won by the great George Pilkington Mills in the big 30 hp Beeston Humber. Both Tuck and Cooper retired in their respective sections of the race.

It is of interest to see how the TT Humbers gradually moved away from being standard production cars. The specification of the 1905 cars was exactly as the catalogue. The 1906 Beeston car was similar to the catalogued 16/20 but differed slightly in chassis and engine size. The 20 hp Coventry car bore no relation to the 10/12 hp (which was a four-cylinder car of 89 mm bore rated at 19.6 hp) at all; if anything, it was closer to the 15 hp Coventry car (four-cylinder of 95 mm bore rated at 22.5 hp) which was not introduced until 1907. An early example of production cars being developed from a racing car?

By 1907 the differences were even more marked. Both cars were entered as 16/20s, though the 16/20 had not been offered to the public since 1906, while a Coventry Humber of this size had never been produced. The TT Beeston car was presumably a modified 16/20, but again the engine and chassis sizes were changed. The

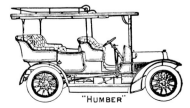

"HUMBER"

A 15 hp Coventry Humber taking part in the climb of Fromes Hill, Herefordshire, in the 1907 trials

Coventry car resembled the largest of the Coventry Humbers but the engine was considerably enlarged, having dimensions of 124 mm × 121 mm as against 94 mm × 112.5 mm. The 'Heavy' Touring cars, however, appear to have been standard 30 hp Beeston Humbers.

The following year, 1908, is perhaps the most fascinating, and certainly the most mystifying, in the competitive history of Humber. For one thing, the regulations for that year's Tourist Trophy effectively meant the end of any hopes for success with basically normal touring cars; something much more specialized was called for. These regulations called for a minimum weight of 1,600 lb (empty), four cylinders and a capacity formula that restricted bore size to 4 in. So for the 'Four-Inch' Races, as they came to be called, Humber entered one Coventry car designed by G.W.A. Brown and two Beeston cars that were a radical departure from any Humber that had gone before.

Gone were the familiar Beeston-pattern radiators, gone were the humble side valves, even the high upstanding bodies had been replaced. Instead there was an engine compartment 'open' at the front with the radiator mounted in Renault fashion behind the engine. Overhead valves with exposed springs and an overhead camshaft with skew gears and vertical shaft drive at the front of the engine met one's gaze. The body was exiguous, consisting only of two bucket seats and a platform for the bolster petrol tank, with spare wheels astern. With their long, raked steering-columns and Humber's own design of quick-detachable, centre-lock wire wheels they represented a much more 'daring' appearance than had Humber's previous TT entries. The exposed engines were protected by a fine wire-mesh cage usually nicknamed a 'meatsafe'.

A 16–20 hp Humber entry for the 1907 Tourist Trophy Race is seen with Works driver W.G. Tuck at the wheel. His riding mechanic is F. Howarth

Our researches have failed to find any authoritative statement as to the name of the designer of these two radically different Beeston Humber entries, but what little has come to light about these mysterious cars points strongly to the hand of Theodore James Biggs. Tuck and Reid drove the Beeston entries in the TT and G.W.A. Brown drove the Coventry car of his own design. None had any success, all retiring for one reason or another. Brown's Coventry car was abysmally slow and he finally retired on the sixth lap with back-axle problems. Both the Beeston cars were much faster than the Coventry car, Tuck and Reid being well up among the leaders in the early stages of the race. On the fifth lap Reid's car suffered a broken steering-arm. Unfortunately there was no replacement steering-arm in the Humber pit, but Pullinger, realizing that the reserve car was lying on Ramsey pier awaiting shipment back to the mainland, dashed off to remove the required part, returned to the depot and got the racing car mobile again, all within a space of twenty minutes. Tuck, after lying in fourth place on the sixth lap was forced to retire with ignition trouble on the seventh.

The two Beeston cars differed in detail, chiefly in that one had a plain vertical-tubed radiator, the other a 'honeycomb'. On both cars

For the 1908 'Four-Inch' TT
Humber Ltd. let its hair down. Here
is the innovative ohc Beeston Humber
driven in the race by Jimmy Reid.
W.G. Tuck drove a sister car

the inlet manifold was a cast aluminium affair of strange 'spectacle' shape, while on the exhaust side each exhaust port led to a separate massive pipe which in turn led to an expansion box. The magneto, driven from a cross-shaft taken from the base of the camshaft drive, was prominently placed on the nearside of the engine front and well protected by a stout leather shield as, with no radiator in front and only the 'meatsafe' as a bonnet, it was very exposed to the elements. The reserve car, which in all probability was the first of the Beeston TT cars to be built, differed in many details from the two actual racers. In this car the inlet manifold was a plain 'Y', the vertical-tubed radiator sat higher and the steering column was less raked than on the racers themselves.

One of the authors (A.B.D.) has been fortunate enough to obtain a great deal of original material from the family of the late T.J. Biggs and among this material was a quantity of photographs of these overhead camshaft Beeston TT cars. Also, it is significant that in a diary, Biggs records that, having moved to Beeston on joining Humber (late in 1906) he moved house twice in the Beeston area in 1907 and then records: '1908 (few months): migrated to Coventry Works, Humber with most of Beeston staff. Address: 63 Dennison Street.' This migration took place in September 1908 so it is certain from this and from the dates in his diary concerning the house moves in Beeston (June and September 1907) that he was at the Beeston Works during the time the 'Four-Inch' cars were in preparation. His photographs reveal that the three Beeston overhead camshaft cars carried the Humber trade plates DU-22-D, DU-24-D and DU-26-D, the first of these being attached to the 'reserve' car, the others to the racers. These plates could, of course, have been interchanged, but there are enough other small detail differences in

A view of the racing Beeston Humber engine for the 1908 TT. Note the ohc and its drive, the exposed valve gear and the unusual 'spectacle' inlet manifold

the cars to suggest that the plates each remained with only one car, certainly up to the time of the race.

The closure of the Beeston Works for car manufacture and the move to the new Coventry factory took place in 1908. On 10 April 1909 Biggs was invited by Pullinger to join him at Arrol-Johnston. As we have seen, their arrival there saw a marked increase in competition activity. Biggs is on record in his diary as having had a substantial hand in the design of the 11.9, 15.9 and 23.9 hp cars that formed the firm's production range as well as in the Coupe des Voiturettes and subsequent Arrol-Johnston racers.

It is also on record that when Arrol-Johnston was busy with these competition cars, all of which were side-valvers, it was conducting experiments (which proved abortive) with overhead camshaft designs. The Arrol-Johnston production cars and some of the racers also had rear-mounted radiators. If there was indeed an overhead camshaft Arrol-Johnston engine at this time, was it inspired by Biggs via the 1908 overhead camshaft Beeston TT cars? Without detailed drawings and dimensions it is impossible to do more than speculate, but it doesn't seem beyond the bounds of possibility.

Two at least of these overhead camshaft Beeston TT cars continued in use as road cars, for a feature in *The Autocar* of 3 December 1910 described the ex-Tuck car converted as a two-seater road car, then the property of Mr Edmund Lewis of Coventry, a consulting engineer and, incidentally, designer and driver of the Deasy in the 1908 TT. Of its performance, *The Autocar* remarks; 'The car on the road behaves well as a touring vehicle. Petrol consumption is satisfactory and the engine is flexible in traffic, whilst its hill-climbing capabilities are all that may be desired, but it

The Coventry Humber entry for the 1908 TT was this car, designed and driven in the race by G.W.A. Brown. It came to grief, as seen here, in practice. Repaired for the race, it had to retire on the sixth lap

is by no means quiet. . . .' This car carried the registration number DU 4182 at the time. A second survivor of the race to be used on the road was used as such in 1912 by a Lieut. T.G. Hetherington, of the 18th (QMO) Hussars. At this time this car was registered LD 6783. It had a sharply pointed prow and had been fitted with an SU carburettor and gravity petrol tank in the scuttle and fairly substantial-looking road equipment. One of these Beeston overhead camshaft engines was fitted in the Barnwell biplane that was built in 1910. This accounts for all three known engines.

It was not until 1914 that another TT race for cars was to be held in the Isle of Man. Progress had been such in the racing world in the interim that the cars that came to the line for the 1914 races (the event was spread over two days) bore little resemblance to those of six years earlier. The TT course was one of the most demanding that could be imagined, calling for high quality steering, braking, road-holding and acceleration. Humber had supported every previous TT, as we have seen. Coatalen and Pullinger had both left Humber for pastures new, though Biggs had returned to Humber in Coventry on 15 April 1912 as Chief Engineer, where he was to design the 10 hp, 11 hp and 14 hp cars that formed a large part of the production output, and also had a hand in the special 11 hp and 14 hp cars prepared for Tuck's sprint and record-breaking bids that were so successful a feature of Humber competitive motoring in the years leading up to the First World War.

For the momentous TT of 1914 Humber's designer, F.T. Burgess, produced a crypto-Peugeot, almost as close a copy of Henry's twin overhead camshaft racers, as were the TT Sunbeams that Coatalen produced for that year. Over the years great speculation has existed as to how Coatalen came to copy the Peugeot design so closely and

"HUMBER"

Seen here in the Works are two of the Humber entries for the 1909 Scottish Reliability Trials. On the left is a 12 hp model, on the right a 16 hp. Both cars have the wire wheels that became a catalogued option in that year

only recently has a definitive version emerged; we would dearly like to be as definite about Humber's 'acquisition' of the Peugeot design. Be that as it may, Burgess produced a team of three of these cars for the 1914 TT and it is remotely possible that a fourth car was built then or a short time later. Race regulations stipulated a minimum weight of 21½ cwt and a maximum capacity of 3,310 cc. The Humbers had a bore and stroke of 82 mm × 156 mm, giving a capacity of 3,295 cc. The building and preparation of these cars was a costly exercise and it is said that altogether they cost the company £15,000.

In the race itself, Burgess drove one of the cars, the other drivers being W.G. Tuck and Sam Wright. Burgess had no racing experience on the 'Island', Wright, a Works motorcyclist, had extensive experience of the motor-cycle TT, and Tuck, of course, was an old 'Island hand'. An amusing sidelight is provided by A.F.C. Hillstead who knew Burgess well in his Bentley days. Hillstead had occasion to remonstrate in a friendly fashion with Burgess over the latter's inability to change gear quietly, to which Burgess laughingly replied, 'That's nothing! You should have heard me in the TT. When I changed gear on the mountain the people in Ramsey had to stuff their fingers into their ears!'

The Humber drivers and teams were on the island well before the race and were frequently out on the course during practice times. There was a wide disparity between the drivers' performances, Burgess being so slow that at one stage there was even the possibility that he might be replaced. Tuck, as was to be expected, was much faster, and Sam Wright, who at first had not been much quicker than Burgess, picked up steadily. It is perhaps significant that Kenelm Lee Guinness, the ultimate winner of the race in a Sunbeam, saw fit to remark on a postcard sent to Nigel Guinness on 2 June; 'All going well here. Our best lap 39 min for the 37½ miles . . . Straker-Squire

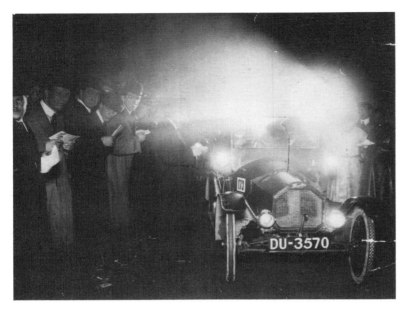

Sam Wright's air-cooled Humberette is seen about to leave the start of the MCC London–Edinburgh Trial, 1913, in the early hours of the morning

and one Humber also very hot stuff. . . .' Tuck's car, No. 13 in the race, was the pacemaker of the team, having a higher compression ratio and a 'ferocious' camshaft, and Tuck himself was by far the most experienced 'Island hand' of the whole team.

The competing Minerva team with its sleeve-valve engines caused much inconvenience, not to say annoyance, on account of the trail of smoke they left in their wake and it was Messrs Humber Ltd. which initiated a protest about this to the race authorities. As a result of this protest a test was held on Bray Hill, Douglas, when one of the Minerva drivers, Riecken, was ordered to drive the car twice up the hill under the watchful gaze of M. Citroen, Managing Director of the Minerva Co., Professor Knight, whose design of sleeve-valves was used in the engine, and a posse of RAC officials under Julian Orde. The amount of smoke emitted was not considered serious enough to uphold the protest. Despite this, there were many unfavourable comments made about the smokey Minervas during the race, though they performed most creditably and, of the six cars to complete the race distance, the entire team finished in second, third and fifth places.

Humber's spare driver, Dayrell, was in charge of the pit, but the entire Humber *equipe* was adversely criticised for poor pitwork, one commentator remarking in the press; 'The firm has a thing or two to learn about modern racing . . .', while at one pit stop they couldn't even find a screwdriver. In the race the cars carried the numbers 2, 13 and 20, driven by Burgess, Tuck and Wright respectively. Tuck,

Closely based on the contemporary Peugeot racing cars, the 1914 TT Humbers had little success in that gruelling event. Here F.T. Burgess' car attracts a crowd when halted during practice

the fastest of the trio and the most fancied, went out on only his second lap with a broken valve. Since to remove or replace a valve involved the removal of the whole block from the crankcase, Tuck's misfortune so early in the race ruined whatever chances he may have had. This, no doubt, influenced Sam Wright when he was plagued with valve trouble on the second day. The positions at the end of the first day's racing were Wright seventh and Burgess eighth, with less than a minute separating their times. On the second day Burgess retired with piston trouble while still in eighth place, leaving Wright to carry the Humber banner alone. He pulled steadily up the field, putting up the fastest lap of any of the Humbers, but persistent overheating brought valve trouble in its wake and he too retired on the 14th lap. So much for Humber's second radical departure.

The outbreak of war so soon after the TT, channelled thoughts and activities in different directions, but the 1914 TT Humbers appeared again in post-war competition. The authors still remain unconvinced that there was never a fourth car but do not propose to enlarge on that. It can be said for certain, however, that one of these cars was raced by Philip Rampon in 1920 with its original engine and later with an aero-engine in place of the Humber unit and termed the Martin-Arab; that W.G. Barlow raced the ex-Tuck car on several occasions during the same period; and that C.D. Wallbank was perhaps the most successful of the post-war exponents of these cars at Brooklands in 1927–9. Burgess took, or obtained, one of them for Bentley Motors where its chassis design influenced that of the new three-litre Bentley, Burgess then being a Bentley man. One well-known car, that of Kenneth Neve, fortunately still survives and

The only known picture of a 1914 TT Humber displaying both its racing number (No. 20 – Sam Wright's car) and Humber's own wheels, instead of the 80 mm Rudge pattern that all three cars wore in the race itself

performs very actively indeed in a manner which totally gainsays Hillstead's strictures on these cars written in the light of his knowledge of the one at Bentley Motors.

We have considered the Tourist Trophy events at some length because it was for them that the two radical departures in the Humber design department were undertaken and also because Humber was the only manufacturer to have supported all the pre-war TTs. In terms of success, however, their activities in sprints and reliability trials were much more rewarding.

Pullinger's influence at Humber comes clearly to the fore once again when considering the firm's successes in sprints and reliability trials. The first year in which the cars not only appeared at a wide variety of locations and events, but also managed to bring home some awards, was 1905. The majority of these were to the credit of private owners and the list of venues extending in 1906, including Australia, is an impressive reminder of the importance attached to such things, even as early as this. As for 'Works' entries, Coatalen himself gained awards with an 8/10 hp Humber at the Brighton Speed Trials and at the similar Blackpool events in 1905, in each case beating more powerful cars driven by more experienced drivers. It is possible that Coatalen was the driver of an 8/10 hp car entered by F.W. Adams in the Nottingham AC's Skegness Speed Trials also held that year.

In 1906 Humber was again widely represented in events such as those at South Harting, Syston Park, Snake Hill, Glossop (an event run by the Manchester Motor Club) and the Saltburn Speed Trials, while in the long-distance events they gained successes in the 5,000-miles Reliability Trial, the Scottish and the Irish reliability trials. The company even produced a summary of its competition successes in the 1907 catalogue under the heading 'Some Humber Successes in 1906'. It was in 1906, too, that another rather mysterious round-radiatored, chain-driven Humber six-cylinder model, said to be of 60 hp, appeared. It was entered by C.H. Cooper for *The Graphic* Trophy Speed Trials in the Isle of Man. What was probably the same car was entered for the Nottingham AC's Speed Trials at Welbeck Abbey in 1907 but it didn't appear at the start.

In 1908 the recently reconstituted Royal Automobile Club (formerly the ACGBI) organized a major 2,000-miles trial that was intended to combine in one event all the competitive elements that a number of smaller and different events could provide. It took place between 11 and 27 June and covered much of England and Scotland with particular emphasis on the more hilly and mountainous areas of the North. Four Humbers were entered, a 30 hp and a 20 hp from Beeston and a 15 hp and a 10/12 from Coventry. As Humber Ltd. was at pains to stress in the lengthy brochure it subsequently brought out about their cars' performances during this event, 'Everything that could possibly be included was made a subject of penalty. . . .', so that the fact that the two Beeston cars were the only two cars from any one stable to accomplish completely non-stop runs was, as *The Daily Telegraph* remarked, ' . . . a feat to be proud of'. Works entries also achieved successes in the Irish AC's Reliability Trials and the Wolverhampton & District AC's new hill-climb at Coalport, Shropshire. On 18 July 1908 W.G. Tuck drove a six-cylinder Humber (capacity not given) in the 'Over 26 hp on RAC Formula' class at the Coventry MC's hill-climb, gaining sixth place on both time and formula. Another entry in this event was a 1907 TT Humber driven by C.W. Hamnett which came in in last place on time and formula.

Pullinger's departure for Arrol-Johnston and the financial difficulties that the firm experienced at the time took much of the 'steam' out of Humber competition entries after 1908. However, the Works continued to support the Irish and Scottish reliability trials and in both substantial successes were gained. Close study of the firm's catalogues for 1911 and 1912 reveals that by careful wording and significant omissions, old successes are being referred to in such a way that only a meticulous reading or a comparison of one year's catalogue with the next make it clear that, in fact, they are the same old 1909 events. The 1910 catalogue devotes three pages and eight illustrations to the 1909 successes; that for 1911 reproduces three of the same illustrations again on one page of text and, by a studied omission of the word 'the' in the title, glosses over the fact that these successes were old ones. The 1912 catalogue compiler doubtless felt that it would be stretching credulity a little far were he to include mention of 1909, so the text and illustrations dealing with successes

"Humber"

Burgess' car found its way into private hands after the war. It is seen here with sketchy road equipment and with the near side of the bonnet open to reveal the twin-ohc engine, *c.* 1921. Happily it is still actively raced today

in reliability trials in the catalogue are reproduced exactly word for word with the vital exception that the date '1909' is omitted. So, any reading other than the most minutely observant one would naturally give the impression that the successes thus eulogized were recent ones.

The annual catalogues were produced in the autumn of the previous year to coincide with the shows, so it was not until the 1913 catalogue came out that the firm publicized directly to its customers the new successes achieved by the make in 1912. Pullinger was by now but a memory at Humber but Biggs had returned in April 1912 and had a hand in the special sprint cars for Tuck, in whose irrepressible charge they did so well.

The new 11.9 hp (referred to by the makers still as the '11 hp'), with its monobloc four-cylinder engine of 69 mm × 130 mm and four-speed gearbox, and the new 14 hp (rated 13.9 hp), also with monobloc four-cylinder engine of 75 mm × 130 mm and with four-speed gearbox, were more up-to-date foundations for a successful sprint machine than some of Humber's earlier offerings had been. Tuck's special car was basically an 11.9 hp ('Eleven') chassis fitted with a very narrow single-seater racing body of somewhat crude appearance (though no more so than many contemporary sprint cars) and the changes were rung between the smaller 11.9 hp engine and the larger 14 hp. Details of what was done by way of tuning and special preparation of these engines do not appear to have survived, but whatever they were they enabled Tuck to put up some excellent performances. Broadly speaking, his speed attempts were divided between sprints and hill-climbs on the one hand and record-breaking and some outer circuit events at Brooklands on the other.

To deal with the Brooklands records first. These were records in classes B and C, the 11.9 hp-engined car in the former, the 14 hp-engined version in the latter, these capacity classes having been newly introduced to Brooklands in 1912. In July of that year Tuck took the smaller-engined version of the special Humber out and captured the flying half-mile, flying kilometre and flying mile records in class B, at 71.62, 71.77 and 70.82 mph respectively, from the Calthorpe that had formerly held them. Later in November that year, with the bigger-engined version of the Humber, he was successful in taking the same records in class C at 75.6, 74.44 and 74.32 mph from the then holder, Crossley. May 1913 found Tuck with the smaller engine now bored out to give a swept volume of 2,024 cc, again attacking the class B records which in the interim had been recaptured by Calthorpe. In this he was successful, beating the Calthorpe's speeds by a wide margin and also gaining the 10-lap record for the class at 76.45 mph. Tuck returned to the fray again in July, this time capturing the records for one to four hours and from 50 to 100 miles held by Arrol-Johnston.

Competition was hot in these smaller capacity classes and W.O. Bentley in the tuned DFP had recaptured the shorter class B records from Tuck's Humber, but these too fell once again to Humber in October. Humber Ltd. was able to announce in *The Motor* of 18 October 1913 that Tuck held every record in class B at speeds from 83.55 mph for the flying half-mile to 68.23 mph for the four hours. Within a month a newcomer to records in this class, a Vinot et Deguingand, had in its turn recaptured the class B 50 miles, 100 miles and 1-hour records. However, the seemingly inexhaustible Tuck added these to his bag for good measure in November, at 75.71 mph for the 50-miles, 75.90 mph for the 100-miles and 75.78 mph for the hour. Some of these fell again to W.O. Bentley's DFP shortly afterwards.

These light sprint Humbers were active in other events as well and not always in the hands of Tuck. Most of the established sprint and hill-climb courses were familiar with them at this period and South Wales in particular seemed to attract Humber successes, such as at the Porthcawl sand races and the Caerphilly hill-climb sprint (the two known as 'The Welsh Double') where the Neale brothers were also active with their Humbers. Up north, Tuck, sometimes driving a sprint Humber owned by Leeds motor agent R. Winn, gained awards at the Saltburn Speed Trials, again held on the sands, and at Aston Clinton and Shelsley Walsh hill-climbs the small Humbers also did well.

Even at the start of his run of successes Tuck had pulled off one

W.G. Tuck, the most experienced of the Humber Works drivers, at the wheel of the single-seater sprint car with which he took many records in various classes, sometimes with an 11 hp engine and at others with the 14 hp version. Its slim lines contrast with those of Tuck

Tuck is seen again with a sprint 11 hp model cornering at Shelsley Walsh shortly before the First World War

second and two third places at Brooklands in the 70 mph 'Long' and 'Short' Handicaps, while in 1913 he took a first and a second at the Easter Meeting and a first and a second at Whitsun using the 14 hp-engined car on the first occasion and the 11.9 hp on the second. His old 14 hp came out again for the 1914 Easter Meeting but it was not really competitive in the 100 mph handicaps. Later that year, in fact at the eleventh hour before war engulfed Europe, he took the 1914 TT car out on the August Bank Holiday Meeting at Brooklands, winning one race at over 92 mph and coming in third in the 100 mph 'Long' Handicap.

War, of course, put an end to such delights and Tuck's old 1914 TT car did not grace Brooklands track again until 1920, then in the hands of W.G. Barlow.

Diversity and Diversions

Many a great engineering enterprise has begun in a very humble way in premises as lacking in impressiveness as a back street, or even back garden, workshop. When Thomas Humber first branched out from smithing to build his copy of the Michaux-type velocipede it is extremely doubtful that in his wildest dreams he could have envisaged the huge and magnificently-equipped factories that were to bear his name, not only in this country but in Europe and even the USA. But if any enterprise is to meet with success it is inevitable that to fulfil the demand there will be a need to find more space to cater for the increased production.

Thomas Humber's first step on the ladder of progress from the most primitive of workshops were small premises in Stretton Street, Nottingham. As his machines gained favour a move was made to Great Alfred Street in the same city, but by the time he was producing his elegant 'spider wheels' the demand for them, brought about by their quality, led to another move in 1878 to Beeston, about four miles outside Nottingham itself. It was here that Thomas Humber established what could be rightly called his first factory, as opposed to workshops. When Humber first moved there the factory employed only eighty hands and, major advance over his previous facilities though it was, it was to expand into an impressive edifice employing 2,000 people in the production of what was acknowledged to be one of, if not the, prime quality cycles of its period.

By 1898 the Beeston Works, electrically lit throughout and equipped with the most modern production plant, comprised of turnery, foundry, forge shop, assembly and fitting departments, departments for enamelling, glazing, plating, polishing, wheel-making, gearcase manufacture, stores of all kinds, messrooms and recreation facilities and finishing and packing departments. In addition there were ample playing-fields and the factory ran its own fire brigade. By tradition it was Humber's Beeston Works that turned out the highest-quality machines, be they cycles or cars, for the top end of the market.

As the cycle industry expanded and there grew up a demand for cheaper ranges of machines so Humber was faced again with the problem of acquiring more production space. When the Birmingham solicitor, Mr William Horton, entered the scene and acquired from the ailing Devey & Co. its 'Express Works' in Wolverhampton, known as 'The Ashes' factory, in Brickkiln Street in 1887, he also acquired the Coventry premises of G. Townsend's 'Wellington Works' in Lower Ford Street and the 'Imperial Works' (ex-Coventry Cycle Co.). However, his purchase posed him with the problem that he had not only acquired factory space but also the poor reputation of their previous owners, a state of affairs that didn't suit his book at all. Nothing daunted, he set about buying Humber's Beeston factory in order to acquire the first-class goodwill to back his now ample factory space. The £93,500 deal was said to have been paid as £21,000 in 5% debenture shares and the balance in cash. In the two months of April and May together (1887) the four Humber factories turned out 2,288 machines but still this was insufficient to meet the orders.

At first Humber's move to the Wolverhampton factory was not attended by marked success. The somewhat unsavoury reputation of its previous owners had left in its wake an aura that not even Humber's excellent reputation could immediately dispel. But within a short time of Humber having put in a resourceful and energetic manager in the shape of H. Belcher its fortunes rapidly picked up. This turn for the better obviously influenced Humber's overall thinking, for whereas at first it had been intended that the Wolverhampton factory would produce only the machines at the cheaper end of the scale, this policy was soon changed and the Wolverhampton Humbers were almost the equal of the Beeston-built cycles, but at a slightly lower price.

The original 'Ashes' factory was extended and modernized so that by 1898 it was four times the size it had been on purchase eleven years earlier. Not only that but in 1896, to cope with the unprecedented increase of trade that the first half of the 1890s had brought about, further premises in Wolverhampton were purchased in Poultney Street. However, events were to occur which caused Humber's Wolverhampton presence to be the shortest of any of its British factory enterprises, the reasons for which will be examined later in this chapter.

The Wellington Works in Coventry which Horton purchased in 1887 were situated in Lower Ford Street and it was to these premises

The body shop, Humber Ltd.,
Coventry, c. 1909. Several two- and
four-seater open bodies may be seen,
as well as one closed body in the
middle distance. In the foreground is
a five-seated, double-phaeton body for
the 1909 16 hp model

that Humber moved to establish its first foothold in what was even
then acknowledged to be the leading location of the cycle industry in
Britain. Here too, as in Wolverhampton, Humbers' arrival brought
about modernization and extension of the factory. It was here at
Coventry that Humber decided to concentrate the production of its
cheaper range of models, a range that by its very nature was turned out
in greater numbers than either the Beeston- or Wolverhampton-built
cycles. Humber made use of the 'Imperial' designation on some of the
cheapest models right up to the end of its interests in cycle production.

Humber's Coventry progress was not to be a story of uninter-
rupted success. By the mid- to late 1890s Humber, in common with
the cycle trade as a whole, was enjoying a boom of major proportions. As so often happens in such a financial climate speculators and
unscrupulous 'business men' were creating a delicate situation in
which the confidence of the buying public could easily be harmed or
even lost. For Humber's Lower Ford Street Works, however, the
setback came from no such extraneous causes but from a disastrous
fire which ravaged and totally destroyed the works on 17 July 1896.

Before recounting how this disaster was successfully overcome it is
worth investigating in what way Humber's expansion had developed
overseas. Undoubtedly this period of expansion in Humber affairs
was linked not only to the general expansion in the cycle trade but
also to the combined influence of M.D. Rucker, who had become
Humber's General Manager, and that arch-entrepreneur E.T. Hooley.
The first overseas Humber factory was established in the USA when
Humber & Co. (America) Ltd. was floated in December 1894 and a
factory was established at Westboro', Massachusetts. This was
followed in rapid succession by the formation of other subsidiary

companies and factories in Russia, the factory being in Moscow, in Portugal at Lisbon, and then in Scandinavia with the establishment of Humber factories in Copenhagen and Malmö. Hooley had major holdings in most of these concerns and was largely instrumental in setting up the subsidiary companies of Humber & Co. (Russia) Ltd., and Humber & Co. (Portugal) Ltd., as well as the American venture.

So, by the time of the calamitous fire at Coventry in July 1896, Humber had reached the peak of its expansionist empire building. It may be added that though the company never officially had a factory in France it was well represented in that country by a large and efficiently-run Paris depot at 19 Rue de Quatre Septembre. Coming when it did, just as the Coventry factory was at peak production in readiness for the next season's range and the autumn Stanley and National shows, at which the 1897 models were to be prominently displayed, the Coventry fire was a calamity indeed. But the rescue operation that followed it was almost a miracle of determined effort and goodwill on the part of Humber's entire Coventry workforce, aided by a praiseworthy unity of purpose on the part of the company management and directors. The undoubted hero of the whole operation was Walter Phillips who inspired those under him with an almost religious zeal to see the task completed. Within an incredibly short space of time an entirely new factory was erected, four times the size of the old one and equipped with the most up-to-date machinery and plant for an even greater production of cycles. Within less than one year of the new factory's establishment it had the capacity to turn out 1,000 cycles per week.

Probably more with the idea of recording and boosting the success of this remarkable achievement than that of celebrating Queen Victoria's Jubilee, the company produced a lavish 'Coventry Works Souvenir' in 1897. Among the detailed descriptions of the factory and the eulogies in praise of Walter Phillips, every aspect of the new premises and output is described. We will content ourselves with just one quotation; 'The central position of the Chief Engineer's office enables him to be readily in touch with the whole of the works. He is connected to a very complete set of telephones by which he can immediately direct his foremen in all other departments.' If this sounds like a telephone exchange operator's nightmare, we think we know what is meant. As far as the plant and facilities of the new works are concerned there is no need to detail them here since such a description would largely echo that of the Beeston Works given already. Now fully aware of fire risks, Phillips made sure that the new factory floors were of 9 in concrete supported on steel girders.

Three outside factors, already briefly referred to, upset the apple-cart, however. Hooley's bankruptcy in 1898 and its subsequent disclosures and the fall from grace of M.D. Rucker and the

Some Humber cars and staff are portrayed in the Coventry Works in 1914

directorate, led to a new Board of Directors being appointed under Edward Powell. A contributor to *The Motor*, writing of Edward Powell at the time of his death in 1919, remarked: ' . . . I well remember the somewhat stormy meeting of shareholders in London, when Mr Powell suddenly arose and addressed the meeting, pouring oil on the troubled waters and offering wise counsels to the much-perplexed shareholders.' Edward Powell and his board were brought up short to face the realities that their predecessors had blithely ignored. A severe cut-back was set in train, coupled with a firm resolve to restore the public's confidence in the firm's management policies and most of all, perhaps, in the probity of the new directorate.

An early result of the cut-back was that the Wolverhampton factories became casualties and were to be phased out by 1901. The overseas factories were also under sentence. Indeed, the American factory had already failed to live up to expectations and receives no mention in the company's 1901 catalogue. Humber & Co. (America) Ltd. was removed from the Companies Register on 18 November 1902, soon to be followed by the Russian and Portuguese concerns.

The next major changes did not occur until 1908 when the Beeston Works, which had concentrated on top-quality bicycles and then cars, was closed down and the firm's entire production was concentrated on Coventry, where additional brand-new premises at Stoke were available. This remarkable feat of re-organization was again the work of Walter Phillips, whose exceptional talents had masterminded the 1896/7 Coventry rebuilding after the fire. So by 1909 the distinction between Humber products built at different factories was no longer needed. Strangely, however, the 'up-market' connotation of 'Beeston Humber' continued to be applied to the top models of the cycle range despite the fact that they, like all other Humber products, were now only built at Coventry.

For sentimental reasons we cannot but regret the passing of the Beeston link and before taking our farewell of it, it is amusing to record some details of one of the last Works Outings from Beeston in 1907. For this relaxation the company issued a lavish little booklet which set out in detail all the arrangements for the trip to Douglas, Isle of Man, on 21/22 June 1907. The large party travelled in three special trains. Even the order and composition of the carriages and dining-cars of these trains, hired from the Midland Railway Company, were given, with a note to the effect that the last carriage and one compartment of the next carriage of the third train were to be reserved for the Beeston Humber Band, whose services were to be much in demand, both on the boat from Heysham to Douglas and at the Villiers Hotel, at which they were to perform during the formal staff dinner, attended by, among others, the Chairman, Edward Powell. The Midland Railway's SS *Londonderry*, resplendent in its smart livery of black hull, white upperworks, red boot-topping, red funnels with white band and black top, and proudly flying the house flag with the Wyvern of the Midland Railway Company, carried the party from Heysham to Douglas. These and other details of the vessel, together with three illustrations of her and her sister vessels, were all contained in the Humber booklet.

The three trains left Nottingham (Midland) at intervals, starting at 6.45 a.m., all arriving in time to take the sailing of the *Londonderry* at 11.30 a.m., arriving at Douglas at 2.15 p.m. That evening there was the staff dinner, for which the full menu was printed in the Humber booklet. This took place at the somewhat early hour of 5.00 p.m., but no doubt with the speeches and the entertainment by the Beeston Humber Band it would have dragged on for some hours, after which there was to be an informal musical entertainment back at the hotel.

Saturday 22 June was left free for members of the party to amuse themselves. The return trip left Douglas at midnight, reaching Nottingham at about 7.00 a.m. on the Sunday morning . . . happy, no doubt, tired perhaps, but surely never drunk.

The concentration of all Humber production at Coventry meant that cycles, motor cycles and cars were all made 'under one roof', a pattern which though by no means unique at this period was, with one or two exceptions, mostly confined to manufacturers on a smaller scale than Humber. Furthermore, Humber was to continue in this manner right up to the time that motor-cycle production was discontinued and cycle manufacture was sold off to Raleigh.

There was to be more startling departure at Coventry almost immediately after the new organization had become centred there.

Humber Ltd. established an Aero Department at Coventry in 1909. Portrayed here is one of the Humber aeroplanes of Bleriot pattern which were available with either three-cylinder engines of 30 hp or four-cylinder engines of 50 hp. The complete monoplane cost £450, or £775 with the more powerful engine. The tail fin bears the winged trade mark of the Aero Department

This was to be a venture into aviation. *The Aero* of September 1909 came out with the following:

COVENTRY AEROPLANES

We are informed that fifty Bleriot 'cross-channel' monoplanes at £400 apiece are to be manufactured in the Works of Humber Ltd. at Coventry, and offered to would-be flying men in England. Coventry, having led in the making of bicycles and motor cars, will thus be the first town in England to take up seriously the manufacture of aeroplanes.

The enterprise is due to Mr Ballin Hinde, one of the Humber directors, who, after studying the different makes in France, has arranged that the Humber Co. shall make a beginning with the Bleriot type. A series of Voisin and Farman biplanes will also be built at Coventry.

Mr Ballin Hinde, who is a Vice-President of the newly formed Midland Aero Club, has recently made trial flights at Mourmelon on a Voisin biplane. The first of the Bleriot type to be put in hand at the Humber Works is made to his order.

Mr Ballin Hinde had sufficient faith in the Humber aeroplane project, of which indeed he had been a prime mover, to set sail early in December 1909 for Calcutta, taking with him a Humber aeroplane and three 'mechanicians so that', as *The Motor Car Journal* put it, 'the aerial education of the great Dependency will soon be commenced'. Perhaps it was Ballin Hinde's pioneering in India that paved the way for Sir Walter Windham's more ambitious project the following year.

The Aero's report was certainly no flight of fancy. Humber submitted a trade mark application on 16 December 1909 and its handsome 'wheel of life' trade mark, already well-known, grew a splendid pair of wings and was adorned with the words 'Aero Dept.' superimposed above the words 'The Humber' on the upper periphery. It became trade mark No. 319,294 registered between 5 and 11 May 1910.

In a nicely produced brochure of 1910 the company illustrated its machines, the Bleriot-type monoplane being offered with a three-cylinder 30 hp engine at £450, or with four-cylinder 50 hp engine at £775, also a tractor biplane with the 50 hp engine priced at £1,100. Also illustrated is what is termed 'The Wing Shop of the Aerial Department' at Coventry, photographed on 10 January 1910. In 1911 a completely new Humber Sommer pusher biplane was introduced, powered by the 50 hp four-cylinder engine. This cost was £1,150.

Humber aeroplane engines were available separately, the three-cylinder 30 hp (108 mm × 135 mm) at £125 and the four-cylinder 50 hp (110 mm × 120 mm) at £425. They were used in a number of other aeroplanes at this time, the most extraordinary of which was the highly unorthodox Edwards Rhomboidal. This almost unbelievable device, alas, as unsuccessful as it was unorthodox, proved to be a total failure when under test at Brooklands in 1911!

An aviation pioneer who was already a man of many parts, Commander Sir Walter Windham, RN, also in the motor trade at the time in question, was certainly another individual in the mould of W. Ballin Hinde who had confidence in the Humber-built Bleriot monoplane. In his autobiography *Waves, Wheels and Wings*, he recounts how, in 1910, he took a number of aeroplanes to Asia and organized the first air mail in the world. The planes consisted of two 'Sommer'-pattern biplanes, one of which was fitted with a 45 hp Humber engine, and six Humber-built Bleriot monoplanes each fitted with 35 hp air-cooled, three-cylinder Humber engines. He remarks that one of the monoplanes was awarded a Gold Medal at the Allahabad Exhibition of 1911. Windham remarks, too, that in the unusual meteorological conditions experienced in the Allahabad region the monoplanes were difficult to fly, having insufficient power. Although Windham is not specific on this point in his book, it would seem that none of the Humber-engined machines was used for the actual first air mail flight. He had earlier praised the 50 hp Gnome-engined biplane and, because of the lack of power of the monoplanes in the prevalent conditions, he does say that a biplane was used. One infers that it was probably the Gnome-engined machine as this was nominally the more powerful. All the aeroplanes had been shipped out to Bombay in special crates and transported by rail from there to Allahabad. Windham was rather sore that the Gnome engine had been sent out from France without any spares or tools, so perhaps it was the 50 hp Humber-engined biplane that flew the very first air mail in the world.

The Humber stand at the 1911 Aero Show. On the display stand in the foreground is one of the four-cylinder Humber engines. The main exhibit is the Humber Somner biplane, and the display is topped by the Humber Aero Department's winged wheel of life trade mark

Pioneer aviation with Humber aeroplanes in India in 1910 was some measure of the technical advances that had occurred since Humber offered a trotting sulky in its catalogue for 1898, a mere twelve years earlier. But even if the Humber Aero Dept. was short-lived (it closed in 1911) the firm's experience in those heady pioneering days of aviation must have stood it in good stead when, in a few years' time, the First World War caused so much of Britain's industrial capacity to be concentrated on war work and the building of aeroplanes. In this Humber was no exception, though it is perhaps surprising in view of the company's earlier experience of aeroplane construction, that it was not to be involved in it again immediately hostilities broke out. W.O. Bentley, in his auto-biography *W.O.*, recalls that at a comparatively late stage in the war he was hurriedly summoned by the powers that be to be told that the senior Humber management was fretting at what it considered to be a major under-employment of its factory facilities, in that it was only turning out the sort of war materials that could equally well be done by a much smaller, less well-equipped and less experienced concern. Humber Ltd., asked if it could cope with aircraft production, gave an assured affirmative in reply. W.O. Bentley was summoned to the corridors of power to be instructed that he was to put the scheme into operation forthwith. This he did, and thereafter spent much of his time at Humber's Coventry Works where his BR series of rotary aeroplane engines was produced and where Humber also turned out many complete aircraft. Among these was the famous Avro 504, of which Humber also built a single-seat fighter version, the Avro 504K. The firm was also scheduled to build, or did build, 850 ABC 'Dragonfly' engines. These were nine-cylinder radial engines of 320 hp. However, by the time the Armistice of November 1918 was agreed, only a few more than 1,000 engine units had been completed from among the thirteen companies to whom contracts had been given, of which Humber was one. Only fourteen of these completed engines had been installed in aircraft out of a total order for 11,000 spread over all thirteen companies.

Incidentally, it was at Humber's Coventry Works that the late S.C.H. ('Sammy') Davis, then with the Aircraft Inspectorate Department, first met up with W.O. Bentley – the start of a significant association in motoring history. Hubert Pike, who later went on to Bentley Motors as head of the Service Department, was also at Humber when the Bentley-designed BR2 was being built there, and it was W.O. Bentley's link with Humber at Coventry at this time that led to F.T. Burgess, then Humber's head designer, himself later joining Bentley Motors on the design staff when the immortal three-litre Bentley was on the drawing-board.

A feature in *The New Statesman* of 5 March 1927 by a writer whose identity alas!, was not revealed, remarked:

> . . . but the Humber people have an engineering conscience and reverence to it. Let it be remembered that in the war, when the Ministry of Munitions and the Air Force were shouting for engines, a windswept corner in the Humber Works kept the lives and freedom of the young pilots in mind. The output people in London might dance and gesticulate and shriek, but never an engine was suffered to pass out of the shed where men leant against the slipstream of the propellors and talked by signs in the deafening din, until that engine had proved its power and its durability.

Although the company renewed its application from time to time to protect its winged trade mark, it was never again, within the period covered by this book, actively concerned with aircraft manufacture. Not surprisingly, however, the firm was justifiably proud of its wartime achievements and sent a large framed photograph of the BR2 engine to all its principal agents in August 1919.

During the First World War Humber Ltd. built the BR-2 engines designed by W.O. Bentley. Complete aircraft were also built for the RFC and RNAS. Here the Aircraft Inspectorate Division staff are portrayed with a Humber-built Avro 504 on 20 March 1919

Aircraft production aside, the company did make some concessions to the changed circumstances of war brought about in August 1914. First, it added models to its range of cycles, motor cycles and motor cars that would have a direct wartime application and, secondly, it reduced the range of its normal products as soon as it found that it was essential to curtail much of the civilian output. Details of these changes are given in other chapters.

In the period from the Armistice of 1918 until 1932 a long account of the methods and processes then employed in the Humber Works appeared in *The Automobile Engineer* for March 1928. It is full of interest but may be summed up by quoting just one paragraph:

> In the matter of Works organization and equipment, the Humber Co. provide an admirable example of the traditional British outlook. Whilst every effort is made to reach as high standard of workmanship as is possible in a medium-priced chassis the result is achieved by individual skill and craftsmanship rather than by expensive special tools, jigs and fixtures. Moreover, the output does not admit of the use of elaborate special equipment.

By that time the Coventry works covered some twenty-eight acres.

A more personal view of the Works in the 1920s is given by J.L. Mussell, who worked there, and contributed an article to *The Humber Register Bulletin* in 1967. He wrote:

> My father, a Brighton man, migrated to the Midlands and was with Humber from 1906 to 1929 as a coach trimmer. In 1924 I joined the

Company as a body-maker after leaving the Coventry Junior Technical School.

The Works, situated in Humber Road on the Binley side of the city, covered an area of 23 acres and was separated from the Hillman Works by the Humber Sports Club recreation ground. The Rec. and the pavilion were the centre of the social and sporting side of the works; I was a member of the cycling club which was guided in its destinies by a Polish, naturalised British, panel-beater named Jack Seigler, whilst the Harriers were a major force in cross-country running having the national champion, Tommy Price, as their star member. The sports club organised an annual meeting where both cycle racing and athletics provided the entertainment, with a flower show thrown in for good measure. Cycle racing on the grass track was a hazardous pastime because the track had a reverse camber at the Hillman side of the ground and the slightest suspicion of damp caused many spills.

The main administration block fronted on Humber Road and in control was Lt-Col. Cole, whilst design was the responsibility of Mr Shorter who had been at one time at Calcott's.

I wonder how much of the influence of W.O. Bentley remained in the design of Humbers. He was at Humber during the First World War and he was able to make the Le Clerget rotary engine produce more power by introducing aluminium pistons. The early Bentley rotaries were also developed at Humbers and W.O. can claim to be the pioneer of light alloy pistons, so perhaps it was the know-how gained in this field that led to Humber using aluminium pistons in the later 15/40 cars. (In fact, Humber's new 15.9 post-war car, developed from the old 'Fourteen' had aluminium pistons from the outset and the smaller model of the range was similarly fitted when the bore was enlarged from 65 mm to 68 mm early in 1921. [But the Biggs drawings of aluminium pistons for the 65 mm-bore 'Ten' are referred to in the next chapter.]

Sammy Wright was head of the experimental department and it was possible to meet some of the old professional racing cyclists who had helped to build up Humber sales, such as Arthur Tye in the cycle department, and I also met Sam Brown who, in addition to holding road records in Ireland, was a renowned trick cyclist.

The main central building attached to the administration block housed the machine shop and presented a confused mass of belts, pulleys and shafting. There was a wide drive surrounding this building which had other shops on its perimeter and at the southern entrance were the boards from which we took the checks which it was required we must place with the timekeeper in an adjacent office to prove we had entered to start work; my check-number was 1070.

At this entrance reposed the fire-station with an ex-City of Coventry fire-engine which the Company had acquired when the local watch committee went over to Dennis motor appliances. There were no horses kept, and the firemen manhandled this antique on the occasion of a fire I saw in the enamelling plant. There was a storage for the Company's historical vehicles nearby; these consisted of cycles, motor cycles and cars, and we used some of the cycles, 'ordinaries' and trikes,

The cycle finishing shop at the
Coventry Works in the early 1920s

when the cycling club put a tableau in the city's hospital carnival procession.

The main body-building shops were on the southern side of the southern drive, and following a disastrous fire which gutted the mill and body-shop in 1920 the mill was now a separate building. The lessons learned in the war on airframe construction were applied to body-building, a very high standard of accurate machining was attained and perhaps Humber were the first to apply stoving to harden the paint in between the rubbing down process; oil-bound paints were used.

I started work in the 8/18 body-shop among a group of other teenagers in a shop right at the bottom of the twin drives. This department was dubbed 'Woolworths' by the senior craftsmen because the production of this model was tooled to such a high degree that assembly was simple and piecework prices correspondingly so low that it was compared with the new American stores that were springing up all over the country. 'Sixpence for this, sixpence for that' was the cynical remark; in fact, my first job was the assembly of the bucket seat bases involving screwing four half-lapped pieces of hardwood together at a farthing a time.

The department making the bodies was in the ground floor of an L-shaped building, the first floor above housing the cycle and motor cycle shops, our shop being immediately below the stove enamelling plant. At the end of the ground floor was the motor-cycle test department where Len Crisp could be found using his very expert knowledge on the 350 side-valve model that held a high position in trials work. The body-shop was at the upper end of the 'L', the tinsmiths' at the lower end of the leg and the paint and trimming shops took up the longitudinal leg.

The erecting shop at Coventry, with side-valve 11.4 hp cars being assembled

The tinsmiths' produced the body panels, petrol tanks and radiators and were, unlike the youths, very highly skilled craftsmen. The scuttle panels and bonnets were of tinned sheet steel and the beaten panels in steel which was protected by the Coslett process of depositing zinc to steel used by John Marston (of Sunbeam) and Humber before stove enamelling their cycle frames, and it was this protection which laid the foundation for the longevity of the Humber, vindicated by those cars now still surviving.

The 8/18 saloon was a small car with little room in the back for more than two children, and the doors, only panelled below the waistline, were prone to crack at the body joints. The roofs were made up from softwood packings above the cant rails and panelled with plywood. This was then painted with a glutinous brown paint and a heavy cotton fabric, known to the trade as 'moleskin', was then stretched over the roof and pressed in whilst the paint was still wet, a messy business, but after the addition of more paint and the rubbing and flatting that was usual, then the roof was a very homogeneous and water-tight job indeed.

A moment's stand-easy for the photographer's benefit in the machine shop, Coventry, in the early 1920s

After the 8/18 came the 9/20 which was a bigger car in all dimensions and was later fitted with front wheel brakes, but finished as usual in mole for the open cars and blue for the saloons, and then the 12/25 with the concealed side curtains which folded into the door. The doors were hung on Soss concealed hinges, quite a tricky job to hang.

There was one factor which came in for some criticism; the Company used Système Internationale screw threads. Those who criticised them would raise their eyebrows now, when we are in the very near future, to adopt the metric thread for engineering products.

I left the Company before the 14/40, but the general appearance of the cars did not alter much for many years. The Company did make some fabric-bodied cars, but not on the Weymann principle, and my father spent a lot of time trying to prevent the ingress of water into the seams where the fabric was joined, causing objectionable odours when the wadding padding became soaked.

The last sentence of this extract refers to Humber Fabric bodies, so called in the catalogues. Where the word 'Weymann' occurs in the title of a model the body was built on genuine Weymann principles.

A further account of the Humber works which appeared in print about the time of Mr Mussell's reminiscences, and from which we have quoted an extract earlier in this chapter, is worth quoting in full.

Like most old-timers I have many varied recollections of the products of the Humber factory. They commence with a sensation in the High Street at Oxford when pedestrians froze to immobility as the Varsity stroke glided along with his feet resting comfortably on stationary

One of the many club and recreational facilities that flourished among the work-force was the 'Humber Benedicts' football team, photographed on 12 January 1912

pedals and introduced the free-wheel to the city. There followed a spendthrift rush for Beeston Humber pedal cycles and the revelation of the difference in quality between £30 bicycles and the cheap assembled £10 machines which had hitherto conveyed us out to Hinksey or along the towpath beside the sweating 'toggers' in training.

The next reel of memory displays Yates and Crundall on chain-driven Humber motor cycles, risking their necks round the ill-banked track at Canning Town in audacious efforts to beat the times of French professional racers, provided by a more generous nation with broad straight roads on which to defeat the clock. Gradually a thin trickle of cars of ever changing design began to flow from the twin factories at Beeston and Coventry, until at last a signpost a mile out of Coventry on the Dunchurch Road pointed the traveller to Humbertown, a self-contained community, complete in itself, possibly the most grandiose effort which a baby industry had yet achieved.

Many good engineering propositions have since come out of Humbertown. The credit for establishing the small cheap car on a sound basis has gone elsewhere; but never from start to finish did the Humber brains make the mistake of regarding the rich man as their sole objective. When manufacturing costs were high, they experimented with three wheels as the poor man's hope; and their Olympia tandem was among the best of its breed. Later came the Humberette, a beautifully made 5 hp four-wheeler with two seats, prematurely delivered no doubt, but nevertheless the source of keen joys to many impecunious pioneers. Quality has always been highly prized amongst their traditions.

One may safely assume the power and trustworthiness of almost any modern British car during its first year. Quality has a knack of emphasising its presence or absence in the second or third year when

Smartly dressed one and all, the Humber office staff pose for the photographer on their outing to Evesham on 28 June 1913

the parvenu may begin to look shabby, or to creak in the joints, or to fail its owner on occasions. Some five years ago one of the early 8 hp Humber two-seaters was chosen by a certain professional man with chambers in town and a cottage and garden deep in the heart of his well-beloved Sussex some fifty miles away. He confessed that he knew nothing about cars, but that the Humber struck him as more of a 'gentleman's carriage' than most of its size. Throughout these five years the small, low-priced car has faithfully transported him between cottage and chambers. Once only has it been late, when a thick fog compelled it to travel most of the distance on second gear, and ice on the road was so treacherous that many travellers garaged their cars and took to the railway; but with the clothes line wrapped round its rear tyres the Humber got through. Only once has the car visited the repairer, when its mistress rammed a hedge in her 'practice' efforts. Today its arteries have not thickened nor its joints grown rheumatic. Its speed is slightly greater than when it was brand new, and its silence is not perceptibly affected, whilst if its panels are a trifle duller and betray a few inevitable scratches, pride has not dictated repainting or the minor expense of re-varnishing.

In the larger spheres similar characteristics stamp all the Humber models. The coachwork is better finished and more ingeniously planned than is usual in each class. If a client insists on a convertible body, he need not dislodge his passengers while he extricates celluloid panels from some obscure lodgement and pegs them into sockets; but his ladies may open or close the windows without reference to him; and when the light screens are in position they will not rattle nor admit shafts of cold air. A glance under the bonnet or floorboards will expose mechanical details which are properly finished externally and look much lighter than is customary, suggesting the use of high-class material for every item. Should fancy turn to a large engine capable of hauling a really capacious and luxurious body, the six-cylinder will be found devoid of 'periods' and capable of providing on demand a few extra horses above those commonly stabled inside these engine dimensions. A visit to the Works will reveal a happy compromise in respect of system. At the two extremes of manufacture stand respectively the individual car built singly, an artistic creation necessarily sold at the figure which such elaborate toil commands; and the mass-production car rushed through by the hundred much as a panel doctor handles a myriad of patients, taking pains lest some serious ailment escapes his vigilance. Midway between the two of them the Humbers are built for that large class of user who desires as much quality as he can afford, but dislikes wasting money on frills. Honest cars of unusually good finish and careful workmanship, they make an abiding appeal to the modern descendants of the old 'kerridge folk' who buy for tomorrow and the day after, no less than for today.

These personal comments and reminiscences ably reflect the remarks quoted from *The Automobile Engineer* and provide a fascinating glimpse of methods of motor manufacture that will never be seen again.

Established Conservatism

The war over, Humber Ltd. resumed motor-car production using two of its pre-war range of models as the basis of the post-war programme. In so doing, of course, it was only falling in with what the majority of established manufacturers were also doing. The company was relying on its already well-proven reputation for high-quality touring cars and was able to go ahead with the immediate post-war programme without the delays and possible teething troubles that the introduction of new models would inevitably bring. The return to peace brought with it the prospects of a great boom for the motor trade in supplying the needs of a public by now, through the circumstances of war, much more mechanically aware. Coupled with this was a new social climate which was more favourable to motoring. To those sick of war and its frustrations and shortages, the prospect of peace meant the pursuit of pleasure, of which motoring in some form was a desideratum for a much higher proportion of the public than ever before. Those car manufacturers who, like Humber Ltd., could swiftly make the change-over from war production were therefore well-placed to take advantage of the predicted boom. Newcomers to the motor industry – and there were many – would need to attract the public to their products. Not that this proved difficult, for so hungry was the public for motoring that virtually anything with self-propulsion, however untried, however badly assembled, could at first find a ready market.

Humber had no grandiose ideas about building impressive new designs based, for example, on the lessons learned in aircraft manufacture in which it, as so many others, had played a vital part during the war. Not for Humber, dreams of a super-luxury car

This 10 hp Humber two/three seater was built for the Humber Chairman, Lt. Col. J.A. Cole, and photographed on 8 February 1919

Cockpit view of a Humber 10 hp, photographed on 13 August 1919

incorporating the latest mechanical marvels like the Leyland Eight; nor even the light alloys and overhead camshaft of Napier or Lanchester; certainly not the sporting image of the Henry-based twin overhead camshaft cars it had so uncharacteristically adopted for the last Tourist Trophy before Europe was engulfed in war. Expediency? No doubt but, as we shall see, not expediency alone. Edward A. Powell, Humber's Chairman and Managing Director of old, might conceivably have entertained other ideas, but he died in 1919, and we cannot conceive that Earl Russell or Lt. Col. J.A. Cole would have looked favourably upon anything other than a very conservative policy. Support for this view comes from Edgar N. Duffield, writing in *The Auto* in 1926: 'I should guess that Humber

An official photograph of a delectable three-seater saloon body on the 10 hp chassis. There was no front passenger seat. The car's lines suggest a miniature of the saloon bodies later built on the 15.9 hp chassis, for which this may have been a preliminary study, as no other 10 hp saloons were built. Photographed on 15 October 1919

Ltd. have made fewer 'signal departures' in their career than any other firm in the British automobile industry. Particularly since the present directorate took office, their policy has been remarkable for its evidence of a determination not to get their lungs in a knot.' A forceful and well-considered opinion by one in a position to know and just how true it was when he wrote it, and was to remain for virtually the rest of the 1920s, will be seen.

The two pre-war models that formed the basis of post-war production were the 'Ten' and the 'Fourteen'. In the 'Ten' the company had a small car which at the time of its introduction in 1914 was a thoroughly up-to-date model and, in keeping with Humber's policy, a very refined car of its size. With its monobloc engine with detachable head and unit construction with a four-speed gearbox, electric lighting and starting (the latter item standard from 1915) it offered more even in 1919 than many of its rivals in the market-place. Certainly there was no falling off in the traditional standard of Humber quality and finish in either the 'Ten' or the 'Fourteen'. The larger car was in many respects a larger version of the 'Ten' with the important differences that the monobloc four-cylinder engine still

Humber 10 hp coupé for the 1920 show. This body style was a standard offering from October 1919, the time of this photograph

had a fixed head (and those splendidly Edwardian valve caps and priming taps) and a separate gearbox. This chassis too, had electric lighting and starting as standard from 1914.

The 'Ten' had been available from its inception in two chassis sizes, the two-seater having slightly smaller overall dimensions and being less 'generously' cross-braced than the four-seater, and this difference continued for some time after the war. Other items that were modified were the electric starting arrangements and the brake layout. By mid-June 1919 the earlier and rather complex CAV system used on the 'Ten' (and shared by the 'Fourteen' and the 11 hp of the pre-war range) which made use of a separately-mounted electric motor driving a universally-jointed shaft, rotating a friction wheel that was brought into contact with the grooved flywheel by means of a foot pedal, gave place to a large Lucas dynamotor driven off the timing-chest. This necessitated the re-design of the drive arrangements, since on the earlier 'Tens' the dynamo, which was belt-driven, had been mounted on the upper part of the off-side of the timing-chest, with the magneto, positively driven, beneath it. To cope with the greatly increased weight and the function as a starter of the new dynamotor unit, which occupied the same relative position as the former dynamo, the front end was altered to give a positive chain drive to the dynamotor as well as a separate chain drive to the magneto below it.

The earlier 'Tens' had separate hand-operated and foot-operated shoes in the rear drums, both of the internal expanding type, and no transmission brake. The post-war version had an external contracting-band transmission brake and a single external contrac-

This official Humber photograph shows the new 15.9 hp chassis, developed from the pre-war 14 hp. The fixed-head engine was still Edwardian in conception

ting band on the rear wheel drums, the former being foot operated and the latter by the side lever. The adoption of the transmission brake soon revealed some lack of robustness in the rear axle department and this had to be suitably modified and strengthened.

As for the 'Fourteen', although it continued as a listed model after the war, it was soon to undergo something of a change, to emerge as the 'new' 15.9 hp. This 'new' car was basically the old 'Fourteen' with its 75 mm bore increased to 80 mm, but still with side-valve, fixed-head four-cylinder engine with the old 140 mm stroke. The wheelbase had been lengthened to 10 ft 3½ in from the 9 ft 5 in of the old 'Fourteen', but the track remained the same at 4 ft 9 in. Since the old 'Fourteen' had shared the same CAV lighting and starting system as already described, something new had to be done for the 15.9 hp car. For this model the flywheel was fitted with a toothed starter ring and a normal CAV starter motor working on a bendix was used. The thirteen-gallon petrol tank was mounted at the rear of the chassis and petrol was fed to the carburettor by means of an Autovac. As on the 'Ten', the braking layout was now a combination of a footbrake working on an external contracting transmission brake

With one mile 'on the clock'! Dashboard view of the new 15.9 hp tourer, photographed in September 1919

and the side lever operating sizeable internal expanding shoes in the rear drums.

This commodious chassis carried beautifully made and finished bodies, the standard offerings being a spacious five-seater tourer and, to be seen at the 1919 Show, an imposingly tall saloon with a V-screen and ample forepeak. Surprisingly, for such a car there was only one door on each side and this to the rear compartment only. This design necessitated a swivelling seat for the front passenger and, all in all, seems rather inconvenient. In addition to the tourer and saloon models, mention is made in the handbooks issued for the model of two-seater and landaulette bodies. Only ten of the former and thirty-two of the latter body styles were turned out in the early days of the 15.9 hp car, though some such bodies were undoubtedly built on this chassis by outside coachbuilders. The decision to market an owner-driver's saloon with no division as used in chauffeur-driven cars was unusual in so expensive a car. It may have been dictated by the strange lack of any door to the front compartment and the odd front seating arrangements rather than by market research into the needs of likely buyers. The landaulette bodies on the 15.9 hp chassis had a division between the compartments and also had a near-side door to the front compartment. Thus there was no catalogued limousine with division (for chauffeur-driven cars) until the advent of the long wheelbase 20/25 model in 1927. This may have restricted the sales of the early saloon models on this chassis to the relatively few who could afford, but did not wish to make use of, a chauffeur.

However, it is certain that some other body styles were contemplated, for official drawings, all dated 4 November 1919, exist,

This 15.9 hp tourer was built for Earl Russell, who became Chairman of the Board in 1920. The photograph is dated 14 October 1919

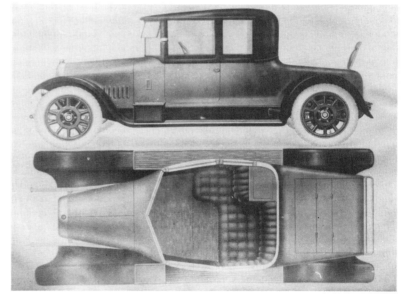

Plan and side elevation of a proposed ¾-coupé on the 15.9 hp chassis, dated 4 November 1919. The seating layout is unusual. This model did not become a catalogued option, though a few ¾-coupés were made

showing not only two-seater and landaulette bodies but a rather strange ¾-coupé in which the passenger's seat was staggered well aft of the driver's, rather in the manner of some narrow two-seater sports and racing cars of the period. There appears to be no sensible reason for this, as there was, as in all Humbers, ample body width and few but giants could have needed the more than generous leg-room thus provided. By accommodating three inside in this way (for there was the usual double dickey seat behind) there would be less likelihood of the centre passenger in any way interfering with the driver's freedom of vision or movement. A few of these factory-bodied ¾-coupés did see physical existence on the side valve 15.9 hp

This side-valve, 15.9 hp with All-Weather body by James Young of Bromley has been in the ownership of the same family since new

chassis, though surviving photographs do not seem to indicate that the staggered seating was used in all cases. The landaulette was the heaviest on this chassis at a shade over 29 cwt, the saloon scaled just under 27 cwt and the tourer came out at 26 cwt 2 qr.

Such then were the models that Humber Ltd. was offering an ever-eager public in the years immediately after the Armistice. But overall, the motoring market was proving to be less euphoric than the pundits had been predicting in the first months of peace. True, there was an almost insatiable demand for cars, but the practical difficulties of transition from a war footing to one of peace brought many set-backs in their train – shortage of materials, labour problems and, most obvious of all to the general public, long waiting lists and a steep increase in prices. Early in 1919 Humber prices were £425 for the 10 hp two-seater, £460 for the four-seater and, when it was introduced, £495 for the coupé, while the 14 hp five-seater tourer retailed at £600. By 1921, however, prices had rocketed to a staggering £600 for the 10 hp two-seater, £700 for the tourer and £750 for the coupé, while the 15.9 hp car was priced at £950 for the five-seater tourer and £1,350 for the saloon.

Humber Ltd., well established and with a fine reputation, soundly financed and ably and cautiously directed, was better able to withstand these difficulties than were many of the newcomers whose existence was short-lived and whose demise was often regretted by few. By 1921 the public was less ready to accept the cheap and shoddy in its eagerness to motor and many a 'new motorist' had learned the hard way the follies of buying an inferior product from small firms of ephemeral reputation and doubtful financial standing.

Early in 1921 a number of important changes were made in the Humber range, chiefly affecting the smaller of the two models. The 'Ten' of 65 mm bore and 120 mm stroke, though still well up-to-date

No All-Weather body was standardized on the 15.9 hp chassis. Here the James Young-bodied car, No. 5973, is seen in closed form. The provision of a door for the driver was a bonus not available on the factory-bodied cars

in 1919 was, by 1921, beginning to look somewhat dated in appearance – a typical 1914 small car or square and upright coupé. So Humber both uprated it and updated its appearance, not too drastically of course, in keeping with its conservative policies. The engine was bored out to 68 mm while retaining the same stroke, giving it a rating under the newly-revised system of 11.4 hp. At the same time advantage was taken to give it a smoother and more modern body line so that it now appeared as a small version of the 15.9 hp car. The old two-seater chassis was discontinued and all the 'enlarged' versions were built on the four-seater chassis. A higher radiator and bonnet line, smoother body contours and a more flowing line to the wings did much to tidy and improve the cars' looks. This was particularly the case with the two-seater and coupé-bodied cars. Mechanically, the most important change was the use of aluminium pistons instead of cast iron.

One of the authors (ABD) has in his possession a rather mystifying set of drawings by Theodore J. Biggs, to whom reference has already been made. They are not dated, but were presumably drawn by Biggs some time during his last spell at Humber Ltd., Coventry, as Chief Designer from 15 April 1912 until he left for F.E. Baker Ltd. (Precision Engines) at King's Norton on 16 November 1914. They show designs for an aluminium piston for the 'small' Ten of 65 mm bore. The drawings carry an instruction in Biggs' hand stating: 'Piston for 65.25 cylinder, 4 off, alum cast', and would appear to indicate that Humber was toying, at least experimentally, with aluminium pistons before the First World War. The 1921 modifi-

For 1921 the 'Ten' underwent a face-lift. The bore was increased to 68 mm and the whole car was modernized, with the result seen here in an official photograph

cations also included the substitution of a Cox-Atmos carburettor for the former Smith pattern, the throttle linkage operated by means of an ingenious pair of toothed segments to overcome the awkward angles involved. On the coupé model of this 'Improved Ten', as the Works termed it, the petrol tank was placed at the rear and fed the carburettor via an Autovac.

Humber seemed strangely loth to drop the old '10 hp' tag for the new model as enlarged, the official photographs still captioning it as either the 'Improved 10 hp' or, for a while, the 'Universal 10 hp', and it was not until 1922 that it became officially known as the 11.4 hp. The new styling introduced early in 1921 was again modified in detail by the time the 1922 models were announced in the autumn of 1921. Detail changes only, but they had the effect of still further modernizing the cars' appearance. The radiator height was again increased slightly, with a higher bonnet line, and the old-style, single-pane, frameless-top, folding screen was replaced with a vertical fixed two-panel screen, the top panel hinged to open in the normal way. A number of smaller detail changes were made at this time. For 1922 a new body style was offered on the 11.4 hp chassis, this being a tall and rather angular single-door saloon with a pronounced V-screen and prominent forepeak like its 15.9 hp counterpart. As on the coupé, the tank on this saloon was at the rear and the feed by Autovac. Whereas the coupé model raised and

The new 1921 coupé coachwork on the enlarged 'Ten' (rated at 11.4 hp) is seen here in this official photograph

A saloon body became a catalogued choice on the 11.4 hp chassis for the 1922 season. It had only one door, on the near side. The pronounced V-screen was an echo of its 15.9 hp saloon counterpart

lowered its windows by means of 'railway carriage' straps, the new saloon was equipped throughout with horizontal sliding, overlapping panes. This saloon body was to remain substantially similar, though with detail modifications, on all the small chassis for a number of years.

The introduction of the saloon on the 11.4 hp chassis (it became a successful and popular option) throws much light on an earlier version that was built on the 'small' Ten but never went into production. Like the 1922 11.4 hp saloon, that on the 'small' Ten of late 1919 had a very pronounced V-screen and prominent forepeak but, whereas the production 11.4 hp and later 12/25 saloons remained angular, the 1919 'Ten' was delicately rounded. It was 'officially' photographed on 15 October 1919 and these photographs reveal it as a much prettier small closed car than the later versions.

Like them, however, it carried the petrol tank at the rear, the feed presumably being by Autovac. The car had only one door, on the near side, and four window lights. However, it was only a three-seater, there being no front passenger accommodation. As on the coupé the two leading window lights were raised or lowered by straps but, unlike the 1922 cars, the rear windows were not made to open. Possibly this pretty little saloon was by way of being a 'dummy run' for the 15.9 hp version to which it bore much more resemblance than it did to the later 11.4 hp saloons. What a pity it never went into production and its graceful lines were not perpetuated.

Even in 1923, Biggs' old pre-war 'Ten' still soldiered on as the 11.4 hp model under the cosmetics of modernization, but that year was to see the most significant change that Humber was to make for the whole of the decade. This was the adoption throughout the range of inlet-over-exhaust valves, a layout to which the make remained faithful until the Rootes take-over, and that company's retrogressive step of reverting to side valves for the 1933 models. If the ioe modification did much to modernize the 11.4 hp, its effect was all the greater on the 15.9 hp cars, the engine department of which had been decidedly Edwardian from the outset.

Not content with this, Humber Ltd. brought out an entirely new small car, also with an ioe engine. This was the Humber Light Car,

A new light car, the 8 hp model, was introduced for 1923. At first available only with a 'chummy' body, this two/three seater model was introduced for 1924. It was a very well-equipped and refined light car

For 1924 a charming three-seater saloon body was introduced on the 8 hp chassis. Of the total of 277 of such saloons, this is the only known survivor

or 8 hp, a charming and refined little miniature that proved to be surprisingly lively. If the old 'Ten' had been considered small on its introduction in 1914, ten years later on Humber could see the large potential for a well-equipped small car that would be a marked improvement on the crudities (albeit linked to economy) of the many small cars and cycle cars that had suddenly blossomed into existence during the first peacetime rush into motoring at economy level. If the new Humber 8 hp was never to achieve the following that soon attached itself to Herbert Austin's 'Baby' (after the initial ridicule at such a pram-sized offering), it must be remembered that the Humber was not really in the same market, being produced in far smaller numbers and priced considerably above the Austin Seven.

The new 8 hp ioe engine had a bore of 56 mm and a stroke of 100 mm giving a swept volume of 985 cc. Like its bigger sisters it made use of a Cox-Atmos carburettor fed from a scuttle tank by gravity but, unlike them, coil and battery ignition was standardized. At first only one body type was listed, a single-shell 'chummy' to seat three adults or two adults and two children. Like the 11.4 hp, the four-cylinder monobloc engine was in unit with the gearbox, the latter giving three speeds and reverse with the customary Humber right-hand change, though in this case and unlike the rest of the range, the gate was 'invisible'. As was now standard in the range, brakes were on the transmission (foot-operated) and rear wheels (hand lever) by contracting bands. Half-elliptic rear and quarter elliptic front springs were used and the little car stood on artillery wheels shod with 700 mm × 80 mm beaded-edge tyres. By the standards of the time the little 8 hp was generously equipped, including five lamps as standard wear when many a small car was

An ioe-engined 11.4 hp two/three-
seater samples the country lanes

content with a three-lamp set, and good instrumentation and weather protection. With a weight of only 11 cwt 2 qr for the fully equipped 'chummy' it had quite a lively performance, a performance which the Works was quite happy to show off in some of the trials of the time in the skilled hands of the irrepressible Sam Wright and others.

The Humber ioe engine layout is reputed to have owed something to that of the ioe four-cylinder Essex of 1918, though real substantiation of this theory seems hard to come by. However, the new models were improved in other ways than by the adoption of the new engine and now all but the little Eights carried the V-screen in both open and closed cars. The 15.9 hp tourer continued the hinged decking with two separate glass screens to the rear compartment that could be ingeniously adapted as picnic tables as well as serving as a rear screen protection or could be neatly folded away. The 11.4 hp tourers now had provision for a rear screen, though the screen itself was an optional extra. These open models also had the rear petrol tank and Autovac feed that had hitherto been the privilege of only the saloon or coupé models on this chassis. The range of body styles available on this chassis had been increased, covering the two/three-seater, four-seater tourer and coupé which, like the two/three-seater

Cockpit view of a 1924 11.4 hp tourer

open model, had a commodious double dickey seat, and the saloon (now with two doors, both to the rear compartment, and the unusual front passenger seat arrangement) and an all-weather with glass wind-down windows, and collapsible pillars and a leather hood. On the 15.9 hp chassis the choice lay between the five-seater tourer, the saloon and the saloon landaulette with division. The saloon model on this chassis now had three doors, the driver's side still lacking one to the front.

The following year, 1924, saw only detail improvements to the two larger chassis types while two new body types became available on the 8 hp light car – a two/three seater with dickey seat and a charming little miniature saloon. Like the open 'chummy' model, the saloon was suitable for two adults and two children or three adults. Magneto ignition was now standardized on the Eights and although coil and battery ignition was listed as optional, it seems that by far the majority were magneto equipped. The two/three-seater sold at £250, as did the 'chummy', and the saloon at £310, way above the Austin Seven class, though no factory-bodied Austin Seven saloon was available as early as this.

The year provided the widest choice of bodies on the 11.4 hp cars, for a ¾-coupé was added to the range. The saloon now boasted three doors, arranged as on its larger 15.9 hp counterpart. The 11.4 hp tourer had the Auster rear screen as standard equipment and the

A surviving example of the 1924 15.9 hp landaulette seen with the roof folded to give open-air motoring to the rear compartment

Specialist coachwork is seen on this 1925 12/25 Humber, the chassis still without fwb which became optional the following year

15.9 hp tourer changed its allegiance to this type, instead of the former decking and separate screens that had been introduced for 1922. Other models continued as before.

For 1925 the 11.4 hp was still further enlarged, being bored out by 1 mm to 69 mm bore, the stroke remaining as before at 120 mm, giving a swept volume of 1795 cc. In its revised version the car was now termed the 12/25, the rest of the range following the fashion by becoming the 8/18 and the 15/40 respectively. The second of these figures represented the brake horsepower, at any rate approximately. On the 12/25 chassis the old coupé body style was discontinued but the other choices remained as for 1924. A major development was the adoption, albeit rather grudgingly, of front-wheel brakes for the 15/40 chassis. Col. Cole in particular distrusted them as dangerous devices liable to promote accidents, expressing himself in forceful terms to an unfortunate member of *The Motor*'s staff for having boosted such things. If Humber had to bow to the inevitable it made

This 1926 12/25 ¾-coupé is equipped with front brakes. This car survives in appreciative ownership

A 1926 12/25 tourer shows the neat arrangement of the hood when erected

sure that its attitude was one of extreme caution. At first, fwb was an option only on the 15/40, and secondly, the method used to link and compensate the brakes ensured that only the minimum braking effort would reach the front wheels. The foot pedal operated the front wheel and transmission brakes, the side lever and the rear wheel brakes. For the new braking layout Humber-Perrot brakes were used, there being a neat little brass plate, in early versions in French, to this effect fitted to the brake backplates.

The other feature for 1925 was a very neat improvement in the stowage of sidescreens in the open cars other than the little 8/18. The

sidescreens could now be folded down in pairs into the specially lined compartments within the thickness of the doors, and when fully folded a neat capping made the whole appearance very tidy. The 12/25 was given a slightly taller radiator and higher bonnet line than the old 11.4 hp cars, but it was still the old pre-war 'Ten' in concept. Balloon tyres were now optional on all models, including the little Eights.

The last year of production for the 12/25 was 1926 so one wouldn't expect any major changes. This chassis now had the option of fwb and both tourer and saloon bodies featured four doors for the first time. The all-weather model was dropped but the ¾-coupé continued. On the 15/40 fwb now became standard, as did four doors on tourer, saloon and landaulette. The major change of the season was that the 8/18 had now grown into the 9/20, the bore being increased to 58 mm, the stroke remaining at 100 mm, giving a capacity of 1056 cc. The three-speed gearbox was retained but the intermediate ratios were lowered. The chassis was changed altogether with a

. . . while this is a special coupé body built by Bridges Ltd. of Cirencester on a 1928 14/40 chassis

The 9/20 model was introduced for 1926. The tourer and saloon bodies were full four-seaters. This 1927 example shows the neat layout of the sidescreens and hood when erected

greater wheelbase of 8 ft 6 in, as against 7 ft 10½ in on the 8/18, the track slightly widened and half-elliptic springing used all round. The car could now carry full four-seater coachwork in open and closed forms. The petrol tank was now at the rear and as usual the feed was by Autovac. Two/three-seater, tourer and saloon bodies were offered on this chassis. In general outline, the new 9/20 was a miniature of its larger stablemates and was to become one of the most popular of any Humber model. In its initial form, from August 1925 until February 1927, no four-wheel braking was offered on this chassis.

The summer of 1926 saw a new model from Humber Ltd. in the form of a new six-cylinder car known as the 20/55. This was the firm's first six-cylinder offering since Edwardian days and became

The six-cylinder 20/55 was introduced for the 1927 season. The five-seater tourer model of that year is seen here

the top-of-the-range model. Despite its conservatism, Humber now realized that the 12/25 was a decidedly ageing design notwithstanding the many improvements that had been incorporated over the years since its origins in 1914. Since the 12/25's replacement was in the wind, the opportunity was taken not only to design a replacement for it but a new top model as well. In setting about this programme Humber did the opposite of what one might have expected of many manufacturers. Instead of designing a new 'four' and then adding two extra 'pots' for a six, it set out to produce the new 'six' first and follow it with a new 'four' that was really the 'six' minus two 'pots'. Indeed, many mechanical parts were interchangeable on the two new models.

The new 'six', the 20/55, appeared in July 1926 and was seen to be a substantial and imposing car, well thought out and remarkably complete in equipment. But being a Humber, it exhibited several conservative features – cone clutch (although by comparison with some it was a sweet one), transmission brake and even the old form of trough and splash engine lubrication. Inlet-over-exhaust valves were used of course, and the bore was 75 mm × 116 mm stroke, giving a swept volume of 3075 cc. Body styles offered were a very roomy five-seater tourer, a saloon and a limousine or landaulette with division. The saloon limousine was on the long wheelbase chassis of 10 ft 9 in as against the normal 10 ft 6 in. This style was the most expensive of the Humber range at £1,050.

The replacement for the 12/25 that was derived from the new 'six' was termed the 14/40, a four-cylinder car, ioe-engined, with identical cylinder dimensions to those of the 20/55 at 75 mm × 116 mm, giving in this case a swept volume of 2050 cc and an RAC rating of 13.9 hp, a very popular size in the twenties. The new 14/40 was to

Fifty of the 15/40 models were the last catalogued of this type in 1927. This beautiful late example still survives

become one of the most popular and successful of any of Humber's vintage products, just that little bit more imposing and 'up market' by comparison with the old 12/25 but very similar in price, selling at £460 for the open cars, £575 for the ¾-coupé or saloon. With these new open cars for the 1927 season came the epitome of Humber's always clever and superior all-weather equipment; sidescreens that wound down into the doors exactly like glass windows, and which could be set by the turn of a winding handle at any desired point between fully open or closed. With their generous hoods and fitted rear screens these cars were perhaps the most comfortable vintage touring cars, even in very inclement weather, to be turned out by a motor manufacturer as opposed to a specialist coachbuilder.

The Humber range for 1927 comprised the 9/20, the 14/40 and the 20/55 'six'. Humber produced 2,507 cars during the year, 1,266 of which were the 14/40 model. February 1927 at last saw the 9/20 equipped with fwb as standard, there never having been an 'optional' period for this fitment on this chassis as there had been on the 12/25 and 15/40. All the range carried low-pressure tyres for wellbase wheels, the old high-pressure, beaded-edge types no longer being offered. A line of the year's models would reveal how cleverly their appearance had been designed, each model, tourer or saloon, on whichever chassis, showing a pleasing uniformity of outline and

Near side of the engine of 1927 15/40
No. 11825

balanced appearance, each reflecting down the scale the proportions of its larger stablemates. Comfortable, well appointed, beautifully finished, built of first-class materials with pride and care – unmistakable Humber products. We have quoted Edgar Duffield before; we leave it to him to sum up this chapter. Concluding a test report of the 1926 15/40, a very representative model, he wrote:

> Nothing about it could be bettered. Everything opens and closes like the case of a good watch. The fit of the bonnet sides is a positive sermon. There is nothing to pinch or scratch even the most careless of inquisitors. Yes a Humber job throughout, amply powered, elaborately equipped and most nicely finished. £645 certainly, which is a lot of money nowadays, but when Humber Ltd. have to fight for business on a basis of price only, Heaven help all that is best of the British motor-car business.

The Seeds of Change

Humber Ltd. achieved one of its better production figures of the decade in 1927, a year in which its recently introduced six-cylinder model, the 20/55, had become the top model of the range and was selling well to those with Rolls-Royce aspirations but not the depth of pocket to realize them, and in which the newly introduced 14/40 four-cylinder car was the mainstay of the range. This model was proving to be popular and successful. The 9/20, that well-liked quality light car, had at last, somewhat belatedly, bowed to fashion in being fitted with four-wheel brakes.

By contrast 1928 was something of a lean year in which no new models were forthcoming but detail improvements were incorporated in the existing range. During this year, Humber flirted with fashion by offering on all models of the range a choice of fabric-bodied saloons, the only changes that were immediately apparent at a casual glance. It is probably indisputable that the finest fabric bodies ever produced were those constructed under genuine Weymann patents either by Weymann itself or by one of the comparatively few quality coachbuilders to hold a licence to build bodies on this system. At the other end of the scale many coachbuilders and manufacturers built fabric bodies in the years when this style was fashionable and one can only say that in many cases, particularly when such bodies were fitted on small, cheap, mass-production chassis, the result was deplorable, even when the cars were new. Shoddy workmanship and poor materials in many cases resulted in these cheap fabric bodies looking decidedly moth-eaten within a year or so of purchase. Humber, of course, produced good quality bodies, but the heavy forepeak and high waistline then fashionable were unattractive features to modern eyes particularly so on the smaller chassis. Perhaps one might find less to criticize on the long wheelbase 20/55 fabric-bodied limousine, but few of this model were sold. There was, it is true, some reduction in weight with the fabric saloons, the 14/40 example scaling 1 cwt 1 qr, 14 lb less than its coachbuilt equivalent.

Beneath the skin, however, the detail changes made for 1928 were sensible and, within the limitations of Humber's obstinate conservatism, progressive. By far the most valuable change was that at long last the old trough-and-splash lubrication system had gone by the board for all models other than the Nines. So too had the cone clutch, a single-plate clutch being adopted, again on all models with the exception of the Nines. Shock absorbers were now fitted to both axles instead of on the rear axle only, as in the past; petrol tanks had a two-way tap and a reserve capacity; and the No. 1 models were fitted with the Lucas pneumatic dipping headlamp device as standard, these modifications applying to the Nines as well as to the rest of the range.

A number of detail changes were made to the bodywork, though here the picture is more complex. For 1928 Humber admitted explicitly to the existence of first- and second-grade bodies, a state of affairs that had previously existed but had only been implied somewhat reluctantly. There was no difference in quality between the No. 1 and No. 2 styles; merely that No. 2 did not include the current year's modifications. In earlier days these models had been known as Models 'A' and 'B', though this distinction did not appear in the catalogues or in publicity material. In effect, the 'B' models were those with the currently updated chassis specification but without the latest body modifications. For 1928 Humber came out into the open and actually catalogued its range as Model 1 or Model 2. Careful study of surviving models and a comparison of the dates that these survivors were despatched from the Works, as shown in the Sales Registers, reveals that in practice a rather less than strict adherence to these distinctions was tolerated. One of the authors (JCT) owns a 14/40 which has all the No. 1 chassis modifications but still has the trough and splash lubrication of the big-ends. The 1928 catalogue is quite specific that the Models No. 2 do not have the body modifications for the year, but that they do incorporate the current chassis and mechanical modifications of the Models No. 1. The new fabric bodies were only available on the No. 1 specification but the purchase of a Model No. 2 on any chassis gave the buyer an advantage in price ranging from £55 for the most expensive of the 20/55 options to £15 for the least expensive of those offered on the 9/20.

Broadly, the body modifications consisted of a raised radiator and bonnet line, a less sharp angle to the V-screen, a fascia board more

This 9/20 model carries an unusual duck's-back body built by Fazackerley's in Australia

This is an example of the 'Model 2' tourer body on the 1928 14/40 chassis. The 'Model 2' had the 1928 chassis modifications but the body was identical to the 1927 version

deeply recessed under the screen, extra body space in the interior, an ingenious 'quick-lift' operating handle for raising or lowering the driver's window, the horn button moved to the centre of the steering-wheel boss, revised upholstery and a deeper overlap of the top panels of the screen. The fabric-bodied cars, incidentally, had flat one-piece screens. On the Nines, the chief convenience was the fitting of a driver's door on all models, and the angle of the screen was altered to give less slope. The Nine tourers, of course, did not have the clever wind-up side windows, but the saloon models now incorporated the 'quick-lift' device of their larger brethren. On the Nine tourers and two/three-seaters a hood envelope was now included in the Model No. 1 versions. An important innovation on the 20/55 cars was the incorporation of the Dewandre Vacuum Servo system to the four-wheel brakes.

It was in 1928 that Humber bought out Hillman, its close neighbour in Coventry, and it was from this time that Humber and Hillman bodies displayed a remarkable similarity. The impression is gained that someone, somewhere, in the Humber empire was beginning to see a red light. Had the company over-produced for 1927? If so, the overt use of the Models 1 and 2 nomenclature was an excellent way of using up the left-overs. Was 1928 intentionally a year of marking time prior to the more far-reaching changes that 1929 was to bring? Were the Rootes brothers already harping on the over-conservative emphasis in Humber thinking? Hard evidence on any of these matters is difficult to come by but it is possible that there were elements of all these factors in the situation obtaining in 1928.

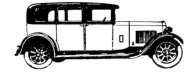

This picture of a 1928 20/55 tourer appeared in *The Motor Owner* in November 1927

So what had 1929 to offer? Disaster on Wall Street for one thing and, we suspect, some unease in the Humber hierarchy, despite the confident announcement of the new models. Production for the year was well up on that for 1928, which, as we have seen, was dismally low, though perhaps intentionally so. In fact the only really new model was a new medium 'six' termed the 16/50 which officially superseded the 14/40, though the latter was still catalogued for 1929 at reduced prices. The rest of the range comprised a revamped version of the Nine, now termed the 9/28, and a revised version of the 20/55 'six', now termed the 20/65. It was clear that the purpose of the revisions to the existing models was in the interests of more power output.

To deal with the newcomer first, not only because it was a newcomer but because it was to form the basis of a run of models that were to carry forward the new Humber thinking and the old Humber traditions well into the days of the Rootes take-over, though the traditions were by then being well watered down. Built on a sturdy chassis of 10 ft 2 in wheelbase and 4 ft 8 in track, the engine

A factory shot of the 1928 long-wheelbase 20/55 fabric limousine. Only eleven of this body style were built

was a six-cylinder with a bore and stroke of 65 mm × 106 mm, giving a swept volume of 2110 cc. In the interests of smoothness and longevity a seven-bearing crankshaft was adopted and the customary inlet-over-exhaust valve layout was retained. However, ignition was by coil and battery, being in keeping with the tendency of the time to use this form of ignition rather than the magneto of heretofore. A separate four-speed and reverse gearbox was retained, as was the open propellor shaft and 'Hotchkiss' drive. So too was the right-hand location of the gear gate and lever and the handbrake lever. Engine lubrication was of course fully pressurized and carburation was by means of a Zenith Horizontal Twin carburettor – rather a thirsty instrument. Bendix-Perrot four-wheel brakes were standard and a brake light was incorporated in the tail lamp, a new departure for Humber. The instrument panel was now indirectly lit and the instruments grouped within an oval framework instead of being scattered all over the fascia board. Humber's characteristic quadrant for ignition retard-and-advance and hand throttle levers had given way to short levers moving in a concealed quadrant. The V-windscreens that had been so characteristic of Humber since 1923 gave way to a flat single-pane screen, and Triplex glass was standard.

From the point of view of appearance the new model was still unmistakably Humber, though a new and taller radiator with a markedly less pronounced angle to the shoulders did much to remove the rather Edwardian tones of the earlier pattern. A similar modification was done on the other models of the range for 1929. Body styles offered on the new 16/50 were a 'dual-purpose' tourer (still retaining the clever winding sidescreens, the last year in which they were to feature), a four-light Weymann saloon in fabric finish and complete with dummy hood irons, and a coachbuilt six-light

For 1929 the old 9/20 was considerably altered to become the 9/28, of which this example is a tourer

saloon. Later in the year a fabric-bodied Sportsman's coupé was added to the range and there was also a two/three-seater open model with a dickey seat and compartment for golf clubs that was termed a Golfer's Coupé, though this does not appear to have featured in the catalogues for 1929. This 1929 version had an ordinary canvas hood like any normal touring car, and the wind-up sidescreens, but was to undergo much change for 1930.

The 'new' 20/65 was very similar in appearance to the new 16/50, so much so that pictures in the motoring press of the time, and occasionally even in Humber's own advertisements, not infrequently confused them. As on the new 16/50, the ioe arrangement was retained but the cylinder head design was much modified to give a more efficient performance, the inlet valves now being inclined and the sparking-plugs moved to the exhaust (near) side. A Zenith Horizontal Twin carburettor was fitted, as on the 16/50, and the inlet cover was secured by an impressive array of brass bolts. This model retained magneto ignition, however. Body styles available on the 20/65 chassis were a 'dual-purpose' tourer, a five-seater saloon and a five/seven-seater limousine or landaulette which, on the longer wheelbase now standard (11 ft as against 10 ft 6 in or 10 ft 9 in for the standard or long versions of the old 20/55), made very imposing carriages. Few were sold, however.

The 9/28 came in for its share of improvements, chief among them the modifications to the cylinder head arrangements similar to the

This unique 1929 9/28 wears a coupé body by Charlesworth and also the wire-wheeled option catalogued for that year

larger models. As on the 16/50, coil ignition was now standard and, at long last, full pressure lubrication to reduce the anxieties in the engine department. The old transmission brake was retained but at least the old external-contracting back brakes had by now been changed to the more usual internal-expanding type. A Zenith carburettor replaced the old Cox-Atmos. Body alterations were in line with those on the larger models, including the changed radiator and bonnet contours. Body styles offered on this chassis were a tourer, coachbuilt saloon and a fabric saloon. Initially, an open two/three-seater with dickey was catalogued but this was very soon withdrawn, though not before a few had seen actual physical existence. Like the rest of the range all the 9/28 cars had Triplex screens as standard and wire wheels were an option at extra cost on all models of the range other than the 14/40. The latter was continued as a tourer, coachbuilt saloon or fabric saloon, these last being, rather surprisingly, six-light saloons and not the four-light of the previous season. The open two/three-seater and the ¾-coupé models were discontinued.

The Motor, in writing of the 20/65 saloon in its Road Test was impressed by the improved performance as compared with the old 20/55, entitling one paragraph of its description, 'Effortless and Noiseless Speed'. But this had to be paid for, since the petrol consumption over varied driving conditions and with an all-up weight of 39 cwt (including passengers) fell to an average of 13.7 mpg. As we have remarked, the Zenith Horizontal Twin was a greedy instrument.

Of the new 9/28 saloon in fabric-bodied form *The Light Car & Cyclecar* commented favourably on its performance, its economy and on the completeness of its equipment, summing up its remarks

Only twenty-six of the two/three-seater body style were built on the 16/50 chassis in 1929. They were sometimes known unofficially as the 'golfer's coupé' on account of the locker forward of the dickey seat which was a convenient receptacle for golf clubs

by saying, 'The public may place confidence in the latest Humber; it is made not only to go, but to last, and the latter, surely, is one of the most important demands of present-day owners.'

If 1929 was to see the beginning of a change of direction in Humber affairs the following year was to point more clearly to the way in which things were moving. For one thing, the main impetus of the company was more than ever directed towards the medium- to larger-sized cars, and what were by this time considered to be distracting elements – the pedal cycles and the motor cycles – were about to be discontinued. The end of Humber motor-cycle production came in 1930 and by then it was abundantly plain that the writing was on the wall with regard to the future policies and outlook of pedal-cycle manufacture under Humber. Regrettable though this must have been to the conservative factions at Coventry, one is forced to admit that 1930 brought about increasing production at a time when many were feeling the pinch, and also saw the satisfactory inception of a new model that was to become a great success and do much to remove the rather staid image that Humber had in the minds of many. The new model, termed the Humber 'Snipe', together with a much-modified 16/50, was to be the mainstay of the car production for some years. Indeed, the model was to continue for more than a decade, even if in so doing it acquired the adjective 'Super' and the not entirely complimentary epithet of 'Humber Super Sleep' – but that was in Rootes days.

For 1930 then, the bulk of production was to be concentrated on two models, the 'Snipe' and the 16/50. Time was running out for the Humber small cars, the Nines being phased out at the end of the year after a reduced production run of only 500. The 16/50 was in fact a very different animal in its 1930 guise than it had been in 1929, but more of this shortly. But without a doubt the car that made the greatest impression was the newcomer, the 'Snipe', a six-cylinder, still with ioe and, at 23.8 hp, rated by the RAC at 24 hp for tax purposes. The 'Snipe' engine had been derived from that of the 'old' 20/65, having a 5 mm greater bore but retaining the same stroke of 116 mm, giving an overall capacity of 3498.5 cc. Numerous other changes had been incorporated in the new engine, including improved inlet manifolding and the provision of a Stromberg UX3 instead of that ravenous twin Zenith. This improved the petrol consumption to 16–18 mpg, even with a stiff new engine, while *The Auto*'s test reporter gave the still better figure of 18–20 mpg. As for the rest of the chassis, which was identical to that of the re-hashed 16/50, a noticeable feature was that the old separate gearbox had given place to an entirely new unit gearbox with 'silent third', but still with the traditional right-hand change. Silentbloc bushes were used extensively and Marles steering was now adopted, while the brakes were of the Bendix 'Duo-Servo' pattern. The Autovac was a thing of the past, the petrol now reaching the carburettor by way of an AC mechanical pump. Thermostatically-controlled radiator shutters were fitted to the 'Snipe' but not the 16/50 models.

A wide range of bodywork was offered, comprising tourer, saloon, drophead coupé, six-light Weymann saloon and four-door Weymann coupé, an identical range to that being offered on the revised 16/50. A special long-wheelbase version of the 'Snipe', a foot longer at 11 ft, was termed the 'Pullman' and was intended for more formal and luxuriously-equipped coachwork in the form of a limousine, a landaulette and a very classy-looking cabriolette (sic)-de-ville, the coachwork on this latter being by Thrupp and Maberly and the price tag at £1,095 putting it well above the rest of the range.

With nearly double the cubic capacity of the 16/50 and little additional weight, it is not surprising that the road performance was by any standards attractive and by former Humber standards sparkling, with a genuine maximum of 75 mph in saloon form. Even more attractive than the maximum speed was the car's smoothness and tractability which made it possible to keep up very high averages without stress to car or driver. Very soon after the 'Snipe's' introduction the motoring press was applying such phrases as 'A much discussed car' or 'A car with all the flash and liveliness its model name suggested'. The new models also sold at a remarkably competitive price, and for what they offered in terms of road performance, well-found equipment and stylish appearance it was expected that success would be assured. In chassis form the 'Snipe' sold at £410, the tourer at £495, the saloon in coachbuilt or Weymann six-light styles at £535, while the Weymann coupé came

The 20/65 model grew out of the old 20/55 but underwent many mechanical modifications. This 1929 tourer model still survives

out at £545 and the drophead coupé at £565. Humber's own bodies on the long wheelbase 'Pullman', the limousine or landaulette, were priced at £775, while the 'Pullman' chassis was available at £495 for those who wished different bespoke coachwork. Chromium plate brightwork was now standard and a wide range of colours was available.

The 16/50 was virtually indistinguishable from the 'Snipe' apart from its lack of radiator shutters, so if you didn't mind the relatively poor performance you could effectively kid the neighbours that you had the up-market version. Even when the bonnet was lifted the differences were not immediately apparent. Prices of most 16/50 models were about £70 down on the equivalent 'Snipe' model, but if you really wanted a six-cylinder Humber on the cheap you could opt for the 16/50 'Imperial' model, available as a tourer at £410 or a saloon at £435. It must be admitted that it did look the poor relation, not having most of the refinements fitted to the other models and still wearing the now thoroughly unfashionable steel artillery wheels.

One of the most attractive body styles offered on the 1930 16/50 chassis was the four-door Weymann coupé, of which this is a fine example

Presumably the sales staff thought that the empire-building connotations of the name would satisfy their customers' aspirations to grandeur. The 9/28, as a terminal patient, received only minor dressings and the prices remained unaltered.

Despite the undoubted success of the new 'Snipe', some criticisms were levelled against it, chiefly concerning the brakes. The Bendix system has come in for a good deal of harsh criticism over the years but still has its stout defenders. Strangely, perhaps, it was not the usual carping at the difficulty of keeping the brakes well adjusted that was held to blame so much as the fact that they were said to 'grab' when applied. John Gilpin, jun., writing in *The Motor* freely admitted that this was initially a feature of criticism of the cars, but went on to say that it had since been remedied, quoting in support the opinions of three (presumably well-qualified) owners, of Humber Ltd. itself and of Capt Irving, then Humber's Chief Designer. Another writer commented somewhat adversely on the strange arrangement whereby depression of the horn button operated the horn in the usual way, but to operate the starter one had to pull the same button upwards, an operation which he found difficult when wearing gloves. Certainly this unusual feature which was shared by the 16/50 models, caused total mystification to motorists and garage mechanics of a later generation. One of the authors (ABD) well remembers the time when he bought an elderly but well-preserved 16/50 Weymann coupé from a garage where it had been deposited on the death of its original owner. Nobody on the garage staff could find a way to start it other than by the use of the handle, and the astonishment was great when the new owner scorned the proferred starting handle and the caustic comments and energized the machine easily and satisfactorily by pulling up the horn button.

For the 1931 season, with the Nines no longer offered, the entire output was devoted to the 16/50, 'Snipe' and 'Pullman'. This year's production was less than that of 1930 and the success of that year meant there were few changes for 1931. The most apparent change was that the traditional right-hand gear lever had given way to central control with a tall and rather massive lever. *The Auto*'s road test reporter complained that it was tucked under the wheel a little too much for his liking and did not 'come to hand' as conveniently as it should. Nevertheless, he also commented that the car's performance was so flexible that one seldom needed to make use of the gears when on the open road. By contrast *The Autocar*'s road test reporter remarked that the new central lever was 'very convenient'. A new downdraught Stromberg carburettor was fitted, with an air-cleaner, the inlet manifolding coming in for yet another modification to accommodate the new Stromberg DX3. Large-hub 'Magna' wheels were now fitted and a number of detail improve-

This view of the engine department of a 1930 16/50 also shows the neat way in which both sides of the bonnet were supported on the bulkhead beading without fear of scratches

ments and changes were made to the bodywork and the fascia layout was re-designed, (a point that *The Motor*'s test reporter considered as being 'improved considerably and the Jaeger instruments, in addition to being of artistic shape with white lettering on a black background, are well-balanced'). One may perhaps regard the expression 'of artistic shape' as being a euphemism for 'gimmickery', as were such other 1931 features as wheels and radiator shutters painted to match the upholstery. However, the 'Snipe' remained a car of surprisingly good road performance, remarkably well finished and equipped and, furthermore, the price for the standard saloon had been dropped from £535 in 1930 to £485 for 1931.

Although Humber had found a steady market overseas in some areas even in the early days, there can be no doubt that the Rootes organization which held sole world export rights was keenly interested in building up much greater sales overseas of the new Humber models. This object could have had no better boost than the fact that in that year, 1931, the Prince of Wales and Prince George used a fleet of 'Snipes', tourers and saloons for their West Indies tour, and the cars acquitted themselves with distinction. Staff members of the motoring journals had opined when the 'Snipe' was first introduced that it was a car that ought to do well in the overseas markets. Perhaps the one feature introduced for the 1931 season that must have facilitated such overseas sales was the alteration to central control from the old right-hand position. The authors know of no left-hand drive versions of earlier Humbers and the only known left-hand drive survivor is a remarkably fine 1931 'Snipe' saloon (Car

The 3498.5 cc Humber 'Snipe' was an imposing machine and no sluggard. This 1931 tourer example is still in active use

No. S.28746) now in Denmark. Australia and New Zealand had for long been 'good territory' for Humber sales, but we know of no left-hand drive versions still extant in these areas.

For the 1932 season the changes were again very minor. On the 16/50 the carburettor was changed from Stromberg DX2 to Stromberg UXB1, the reverse trigger rod that protruded through the knob of the gear lever was dispensed with, the reverse position being protected by a spring-loaded plunger. The Bendix Duo-Servo brakes were now cable-operated instead of by rods, the hub knave plates had a different method of fixing (the earlier press-fit pattern had a habit of detaching themselves), the instrument panel was again re-designed (with the result that 1931 instruments could not be fitted on 1932 cars) and the steering wheel and controls were finished in black, instead of the brown of 1931. On the 'Pullman' the radiator height was increased by 2 in to accord with this model's re-designed bonnet and bodywork. A new clutch was incorporated in all the 1932 models.

It was from 1932 that the Rootes organization had actually become a manufacturing combine, so that for the new models announced for 1933 it saw fit to abandon the inlet-over-exhaust design that had served Humber so well from its introduction in 1923 and reverted to flat-head side-valves. A new four-cylinder car was introduced, the Twelve, again, of course, with a side-valve engine. The 16/50 now became the side-valve 16/60 and the 'Snipe' became the 'Snipe 80', though the 'Pullman' remained the same. In the ensuing years many strange permutations between Humber, Hillman and Talbot (later Sunbeam-Talbot), which had all been taken under the Rootes umbrella, were to be found. Those who, like Georges Roesch of Talbot, had designed thoroughbred cars of high quality, were

This 1931 'Snipe' in saloon form was exported to Denmark and is the only known left-hand drive survivor of the marque

disgusted at the degree of expediency and badge engineering that increasingly became evident and severed their connections with the cars concerned. It is a sad but true reflection that much of the ethos that governed the affairs of Humber from the earliest days in the cycle trade went out of the window along with the ioe engines after 1932. With the pedal cycles now under the wing of Raleigh it was doubly unfortunate that the same sorry tale was repeated there, Humber machines being Humber only in name and with nothing left to them of their once proud, indeed superlative, heritage.

The Humber Register

Although interest in 'old' cars goes back many years to the beginnings of the Veteran Car Club of Great Britain and the Vintage Sports Car Club in the 1930s, and 'one-make' clubs such as those for Jowett or Riley can claim even earlier origins, it is only in comparatively recent years that 'one-make' clubs have proliferated.

In the early 1950s there was little collective interest in older cars that had no sporting pretensions or were not old enough to be classed as 'Veterans'. One of the authors (ABD) had at that time owned several early sports cars and then fell to the charms of a 1924 11.4 Humber saloon offered for sale by its original owner. That original owner happened to come from a family with long and renowned associations with Humber products, for the owner's father was none other than the great Herbert Synyer of Nottingham who had raced Humber 'Ordinaries' with conspicuous success in the 1880s.

The quality of this car so impressed itself upon its new owner that he decided that there must be other owners of Humbers who would benefit by being brought together informally by the formation of a club or register. Letters to the motoring press followed and with a preliminary target of twenty-five interested persons to make the effort worthwhile, the notion of such a club was formulated. Its inaugural meeting was held (with a wry sense of humour) on 1 April 1951 and was attended by ten vintage Humbers, their owners and friends. The enthusiasm, friendship and appreciation of the cars' worth (in other than financial terms) were clearly evident and more ambitious things were then contemplated. Within six weeks another

Members of the Humber Register have made some rare discoveries. Here are the remains of the only known 1908 30 hp six-cylinder Coventry Humber, discovered in Australia and now undergoing restoration

They have also tackled some formidable restoration jobs. This abandoned 1928 9/20 saloon is now fully restored and in use

event had been staged and both this and the inaugural meet had been given some coverage by the motoring press.

From then on things went from strength to strength and within two years the membership had reached three figures. Further events were held, a technical library was started from which members could have material on loan and a simple News Sheet was circulated to keep members in touch and abreast of events and matters of Humber interest. By 1957 the Register had become too time-consuming to be dealt with as a solo effort as it had been up to that time and a proper Committee, Registrar and Treasurer were appointed, together with

An imposing array of members' cars at one of the Humber Register's 1988 events

individuals who would provide technical expertise for specific models. It was also felt that proper measures should be put in hand to ensure a supply of new and second-hand spares.

John Tarring, who became a member of the Register in 1958, took the historical side into his care, painstakingly amassing over the years an ever-increasing stock of archive material, records and photographs which has proved invaluable in assisting in the accurate restoration of members' cars in many parts of the world. The search for this material is on-going and 'new' items still come to light from time to time.

W.S. (Bill) May took over the Registrar's duties, to be followed successively by Michael Hall, Phil Diffey and Hugh Gregory, the present incumbent, to all of whom a real debt of gratitude is owed for their loyal and enthusiastic service. The infant spares scheme was brought to fruition by Douglas Irvine and flourished under Geoff Hare, John Kirkby and Hugh Gregory, the present Spares Registrar, so that today the Register can offer as comprehensive a spares-availability service as probably any one-make club of comparable size.

Members' cars are not just for spit-and-polish parades, as this shot of a 1928 9/20 saloon taking part in a recent VSCC event clearly shows

Sometimes a lucky discovery brings to light a rare model in totally original condition. This is a 1920 15.9 hp saloon, No. 4658, found with only 10,000 miles to its credit and last on the road in 1924, before its resurrection more than sixty years later

Successive Competition Secretaries, the present incumbent being Lt. Col. R.N. (Dick) Arman, have maintained an active programme of events, among them those that compete with allied one-make clubs that form the Inter-Register Club, a body of clubs that gives its members some say in the overall concerns of veteran and vintage motoring, particularly its standing in the ever-increasing welter of official legislation of one kind or another. The register now has a

Views of the sumptuous interior bear out No. 4658's remarkable originality

membership of 270, with members in Australia, Austria, Denmark, Eire, France, Holland, Italy, Madeira, New Zealand, Norway, South Africa, Spain, Switzerland, Sweden and the USA.

Notable landmarks in the Humber Register's history have been the Centenary Rally held at the Humber Works in 1968 to celebrate 100 years since Thomas Humber inaugurated the business, and Twenty-First and a Silver Jubilee events specially marking these steps in the club's existence since its inception in 1951.

It remains a source of some amazement, as well as one of great satisfaction, that today, some thirty-eight years since the Register was founded, 'new', and in some cases, very rare Humber survivors come to the surface. In Australia, for example, the only known example of the very rare 30 hp six-cylinder Coventry model of 1908/9 has come to light very recently, while in this country an example of the side-valve 15.9 hp saloon, introduced for the 1920 season, has been discovered. This example was last used on the road in the mid-1920s and has covered less than 10,000 miles altogether. It exhibits many detail features that differ from the catalogued specification but are obviously authentic, proving once again how difficult it is for any historian to be totally dogmatic about what was and what wasn't. A great deal of circumstantial 'evidence' has come to light to suggest that there is a strong possibility there were four, and not three, of the crypto-Peugeot 1914 TT Humber racing cars, but here again to be dogmatic is impossible. Unchanging, however, is the evidence of the quality that went into all the pre-Rootes Humber products, and the keenness, enthusiasm, dedication and friendliness of the members of the Humber Register who keep 'alive' in physical shape the products of the Humber name.

Over all these years the 1924 11.4 saloon that was the inspiration for the Register's existence has gone motoring steadily on and, having by now covered a staggering total mileage, is still very active in a member's hands in Sweden. A worthwhile testimony to the quality of the product.

A line drawing by George Oliver portrays the only known surviving example of the 11.4 hp All-Weather model, No. 2080. This was a catalogued body on the 11.4 hp chassis, continued for one year only on the 12/25

Appendix I : Company

The Company : Changes in Title

Like many long-established firms, the company underwent numerous financial and boardroom reconstructions.

(1)	Thomas Humber, Bicycle Manufacturer	1868 (?)–75	
(2)	Humber & Marriott	1875–7	
(3)	Humber, Marriott & Cooper	1877–85	
(4)	Humber & Co.	1885–7	
		Incorporated	*Wound up*
(5)	Humber & Co. Ltd.	6 June 1887	13 January 1888
(6)	Beeston Humber Cycle Manufacturing Co. Ltd.	6 June 1887	29 November 1907
(7)	Humber Manufacturing Co. Ltd.	6 June 1887	29 November 1907
(8)	The Humber Cycle Co. Ltd.	10 June 1887	27 November 1907
(9)	Humber & Co. Ltd.	14 June 1887	7 November 1897
(10)	Humber & Co. Ltd.	23 November 1896	7 November 1906
(11)	Humber & Co. (Extension) Ltd.	26 March 1896	7 November 1906
(12)	Humber Ltd.	8 March 1900	17 February 1909
(13)	Humber Ltd.	17 February 1909	

The Company : Overseas Subsidiaries

	Incorporated	*Wound up*
Humber & Co. (America) Ltd.	11 December 1894	18 November 1902*
Factory: Westboro', Mass.		
Main Depot: 318, Broadway, New York.		
Humber & Co. (Russia) Ltd.	16 August 1895	19 May 1905*
Factory: Moscow		
Humber & Co. (Portugal) Ltd. (i)	5 October 1895	7 October 1904*
Factory: Lisbon		
Humber & Co. (Portugal) Ltd. (ii)	23 November 1899	17 June 1904
Factory: Lisbon		
Humber & Co. (Denmark) Ltd.	1897	
Factory: Copenhagen		
Humber & Co. (Sweden) Ltd.	1897	1900. Taken over by Maskinfabriksaktiebologet Scania, Malmo. Registered 16 April 1901
Factory: Malmo		

  * Removed from *The Companies Register*

The Company : British Factories

Nottingham	: Stretton Street	1870
	Queen's Road	1875
Beeston	:	1878 greatly extended.
		Closed 1908
Coventry	: Lower Ford Street	1887 (ex-Gorton & Co.)
	(burnt down 17 July 1896)	
	New factory rebuilt under Walter Phillips	
	Stoke	1908
Wolverhampton	: 'The Ashes', Brickkiln Street	1887 (ex-Devey & Co.)
	'The Ashes'	Closed 1900
	Poultney Street : 1896	Closed 1900

The Company : British Subsidiary

	Incorporated	Wound up
Humber & Co. (Extension) Ltd.	26 March 1896	1906*

* Removed from *The Companies Register*

The Company: British Depots

London	: Lillie Road	opened under F. Cooper
	32 Holborn Viaduct	1889 onwards
Repair Depot	: Canterbury Road, Kilburn, NW	1914–21
Export Depot	: Humber House, 94 New Bond Street, W1	1923–9 (now termed Export Branch Office)
Birmingham	: 4 Victoria Square	1902–06
	280 Broad Street	1907–10
Brighton	: 68 Preston Street	1897
	66/68 Preston Street	1898–1902
Leeds	: 2 New Station Street	1890
Liverpool	: 73 Bold Street	1902–05
	27 & 33 Leece Street	1906
Manchester	: 5 Deansgate	1902–06
	31/33 Blackfriars Street	1907–11
Nottingham	: 19 Wheelergate	1902–04
	Grey Friar Gate	1905–11
Stourbridge	Oldswinford	1904
Southampton	: 113 Above Bar	1901
	27 London Road	1902–14
	25 & 27 London Road	1915–21

Notes on the Major Factories

BEESTON

Originally employed some eighty hands. By 1898 employed about 2,000 hands. At this date it was electrically lit throughout and comprised of offices, stores, mess-rooms, turnery, foundry, forge shop, assembly and fittings departments, together with departments for enamelling, glazing, plating, polishing, wheel-making, gearcase manufacture, stores for rims and wheels and finishing and packing departments. There was a large recreation ground, playing fields, recreation club room and the factory ran its own fire brigade. Closed in 1908.

WOLVERHAMPTON

The Wolverhampton enterprise did not at first prosper, perhaps because its former occupants, J. Devey & Co., had been in troubled waters and Devey himself in trouble with the law. Efficient new management turned the scale. 'The Ashes' factory was enlarged, the six erecting shops occupying some 15,000 sq ft, other departments being equally spacious. The finishing shop had a floor area of 3,000 sq ft. The Poultney Street factory was acquired as an 'overflow' when demand rapidly increased in the boom years of the 1890s.

COVENTRY

Following the disastrous fire at the Lower Ford Street Works in July 1896, H.J. Lawson, the 'motor' magnate and financier, who was at the time involved with getting Humber & Co. Ltd. interested in his schemes for motor manufacture, made available temporary factory space in the old 'Cotton Factory' which became 'The Motor Mill'. Under Walter Phillips' supervision new land was acquired and a new larger factory built in an incredibly short space of time on the same site. The new factory was four times the size of its predecessor, with a floor area of 80,000 sq ft. With the fire disaster fresh in his mind, Phillips had the floors of the new factory constructed of 9 in concrete on steel girders. By 1898 it was turning out 1,000 cycles per week. A pleasing remark states: 'The central position of the Engineer's office enables him to be readily in touch with the whole of the Works. He is connected to a very complete set of telephones by which he can immediately direct his foremen in all other departments.'

Humber & Co., Paris

19, Rue du 4 Septembre, Paris, 19

Although classed as a depot it enjoyed a considerably higher status than that afforded to any of its British counterparts, being almost akin to the later-established Humber & Co. (Extension) Ltd. of London. French Humber machines carried a modified version of the Humber trade mark, on which the words 'Paris' and the address appeared superimposed upon the outer upper periphery of the badge, an elaboration not accorded to any of the machines supplied by any of the British depots. The 'Directeur de Humber et C° en France' was F. Charron, later to make a name for himself in the motor racing and motor manufacturing fields. Martin D. Rucker was 'Le Directeur general'.

Appendix II: Cycles

Aids to Identification

(A) FRAME DETAILS

(i)   *Duplex Chainstay* (on the driving (off) side)
Fitted to Beeston Humbers. Introduced: 1897
Not shown in (abridged) 1902 catalogue, but fitted to Beeston Humber Gentleman's Racer Model No. 4 (1904): No. 3 (1905)

(ii)   *Brazeless Joints* (Patent Nos. 24564/1896; 25025/1896; 29715/1896) Introduced: 1897
Normal brazed frames continued as an option. Brazeless joint frames gradually discontinued, probably due to lack of demand, except on aluminium-framed machines. An aluminium-framed model was catalogued until 1908.

(iii)   *Beeston Humber Duplex Front Fork*: Reg. No. 322081
          Introduced on all Beeston models, 1900. Continued in use on Beeston models right up to the Raleigh take-over, after which its use was extended to a wider range of models.
(iv)   *Swing Chain Adjustment* Introduced: 1892
(v)   *Combined Crank and Chainwheel* Introduced: 1895
(vi)   *Crank & Chainwheel Separate* Introduced: 1896
(vii)   *Trade mark ('Wheel of Life') Chainwheel*
          Introduced on Beeston Humbers in 1902. Use extended to most models in the range in 1904. Exceptions were: juvenile models, models, usually racers, fitted with a high gear and very large chainwheel and 'Olympia' models (until 1923).
(viii)   *Beeston Humber Ladies' Duplex Frame*
          (a)   Straight-tube type: Reg. No. 368099 introduced 1904. Discontinued for 1906.
          (b)   Curved-tube type: Reg. No. 374732 introduced 1902. Discontinued for 1907.
          (c)   Duplex curved top down tubes only: Reg. No. 472213 introduced 1908.
(ix)   *Gents' Single-Tube Cross Frame* (similar to the Raleigh design)
          Introduced: 1923. Catalogued 1925. Not catalogued 1929. (A Dutch catalogue of 1936 lists the cross-frame model exactly as Raleigh, even to Raleigh front forks and fork crown, but this model is not listed in the British 1936 catalogue.)
(x)   *Other Cross Frame Models* (Duplex tubes running from top of steering head to bottom bracket, the single tube from the top of the seat tube to the bottom of the steering head passing between the duplex tubes.)
          Introduced: 1902. Fitted to Beeston Humber Gents' models and to First Grade Gents' Light Roadsters. A diamond-frame option was catalogued in each case. Also First Grade Humber Road Racer Model No. 16.
(xi)   *Spring Frame Models*
          (a)   1896: Ladies' & Gents' model
          (b)   1902: Beeston Humber Gents' Model No. 27 and Standard 'Special' Model No. 28
(xii)   *Humber-Pedersen 'Cantilever' Frame* Introduced: 1898 (Beeston-made)
(xiv)   *Humber 'Chainless' Safety* (Beeston-made, under Acatène license)
          Introduced: 1898

(B) VARIABLE GEARS

(i)   *Two-Speed Hub Gears*
          1900:   Offered as an option on Beeston 'Modèles d'Or' at no extra cost.
          1904:   A catalogued option at £2 10s (£2.50). £2 15s (£2.75) if fitted to machines with band brakes on rear wheel.
          1905:   A catalogued option at no extra charge on Beeston models; extra charges as 1904 for other models.
          1906:   Catalogued on two models, but available as for 1905 if a preferred option to the newly introduced Humber-Cordner three-speed hub gear.
          1909 and 1910:   Catalogued as only available on the Ladies' and Gents' tricycles.
(ii)   *Three-Speed Hub Gears*
          Humber-Cordner gear introduced for 1906 range. Direct drive on middle gear, 27 per cent reduction, 31 per cent increase.
          1906:   Humber-Cordner (1st pattern: rod and bell-crank operation). Catalogued on three models, optional extra on seven models.
          1907:   Humber-Cordner (1st pattern: wire and pulley operation).
          1908:   Humber-Cordner (revised pattern: wire and pulley operation).
          1909:   Sturmey-Archer. Direct drive on middle gear, 23¾ per cent reduction and 31¼ per cent increase. Sturmey-Archer variable gears remained the catalogued gears from 1909 right through to the end of Humber's independent cycle production in 1932, though other types of variable gears could be fitted as an option at extra cost.

(C) CHAIN PITCHES

Pre-1897:   1 in pitch block chains.

1897:   Beeston and Wolverhampton models. ⅝ in pitch roller chains. Coventry models had 1 in pitch block chains.

1900:   Beeston & 1st Grade models had ⅝ in pitch roller chains. Standard models had 1 in block chains. Standard fixed wheel and Standard free-wheel Road Racers had 1 in pitch double roller chains.

1901:   ⅝ in pitch roller standard throughout range.

1906:   Standard Special Gents' Road Racer had ⅝ in × ⅛ in roller chain; no details given for other models.

1913:   All Beeston models and Light Club and Road Racer models had ⅝ in × ⅛ in roller chains. No details given for other models.

1914/15:   As 1913.

Post-war: ½ in pitch roller standard throughout the range.

(D) BRAKES

A difficult topic to sort out with any degree of clarity. In common with most makers, early machines that were fitted with brakes usually made use of the spoon brake acting on the front tyre. Many Gents' racers and Light Roadsters were not fitted with any brakes. Braked models that were an *exception* to the front-spoon type were:

1889:   Beeston Humber Models 1 and 4; spoon brake acting on *rear* tyre.

1895:   1898 Tandem Model I (lady front, small front wheel) had spoon brake on *rear* tyre.

Pneumatic front spoon brake: an option on any 1898 model, including those with dropped handlebars.

(a)   *Band brakes* Patent Nos: 16795/1892; 17484/1899; 19901/1899; 1987/1902.

     (i)   On tricycles: Hand lever operated; 1887–1909. Band acting on drum on main axle.

     (ii)   On safeties: Back-pedal operated; 1900–1906.

     (iii)   On safeties: Band brake acting on *front* wheel, hand-lever operated, available at extra cost on the following models:

        1892 Beeston Humber No. 1 Safety.

        1894 Beeston Humber No. 1 and No. 2 Safeties.

(b)   *Rim brakes*

     (i)   Front wheel, hand-lever operated: 1900; on all safeties except fixed-wheel 'Standard' model (spoon brake) and brakeless models (racers) and tricycles (band brake on main axle).

     (ii)   Front wheel, thumb-lever operated: 1901 option for light machines or for those with dropped handlebars.

     (iii)   Roller lever operated: 1904; except 'Standard' models. 1905 onwards, throughout the range except those models listed below under different categories.

     (iv)   Rear wheel rim brakes: back-pedal operated: 1900 and 1901 on those machines not fitted with the band brake option.

     (v)   Rear wheel rim brake; inverted lever cable operated: 1902 on those machines not fitted with band brake option. 1904 on 'Standard' model only as option to back-pedal band brake.

(c)   *Coaster brakes; rear hub*

     1910   :   Special Road Racer

     1911   :   ″   and on 'Light Club' model

     1912   :   ″   ″

     1913   :   ″   ″

     1914   :   ″   ″

     1915   :   ″   ″

(d)   *Cable-operated Caliper rim brakes*:

     1925   :   Road Racer, to rear wheel only.

     1929   :   'The Club' model, to rear wheel only.

Within this general framework there were so many options that it is difficult to be dogmatic as to what any one individual machine might have, but the details given here, all ex-catalogue, should serve as a useful guide as to what was available in the range in any year.

(E) WHEELS & TYRES

(i) *Spokes*

Thomas Humber had a rooted objection to the use of tangent spokes and would not countenance them during his active time with the company. All models, pre-1893, therefore had direct (radial) spokes.

1893/4 'Semi-tangent' spokes (tangent on driving (off) side, direct on near side) introduced for some models. Front wheel spokes still direct on all models.

1895 Tangent spokes to front and rear wheels on all but the cheapest models of the range.

1896 and subseqently. Tangent spokes throughout.

(ii) *Wheel sizes*

In all cases the *rear* wheel size is the first mentioned, irrespective of whether the rear is the driven wheel or not. 'Ordinaries' when listed had the usual options as to wheel sizes, in 2 in steps, and no futher details will be given here as to 'Ordinary' wheel sizes.

1889: Gents' Safeties; 30/30 in except No. 1 (30/24 in).
  Juvenile machines; equal to suit size (24/24 in or 26/26 in).
  Juvenile tricycles; No. 10 26/22 in: No. 11 30/24 in: No. 12 36/26 in.
  Adult tricycles; No. 0 40/22 in: No. 1 30/24 in: No. 2 36/22 in: No. 5 30/26 in: No. 6 30/26 in: No. 7 30/26 in: No. 8 30/26 in.
  Tandem tricycles; No. 5 24/40 in: No. 6 24/40 in: No. 7 18/44 in.

1890: Gents' Safeties; 30/30 *except* : No. 2 28/30 in: No. 6 28/30 in: No. 7 28/30 in: No. 8 (Ladies') 26/26 in.
  Tricycles; 30/26 in *except* No. 1 30/24 in and No. 3 30/24 in and Juvenile machines.
  Tandem Tricycles; 36/26 in: No. 12 24/40 in.

1892: Safeties; 28/30 in *except* No. 8 26/28 in.
  Tricycles; 28/28 in *except* No. 22 26/26 in: No. 23 26/28 in: No. 37 26/28 in: No. 38 26/28 in.
  Tandems; No. 17 24/36 in.

1894: Safeties; Gents' 28/30 in: Ladies' 26/28 in.
  Tricycles; 26/26 in.

1895: Safeties; Gents' 28/30 in: Ladies' 26/28 in: Youths' 26/26 in: Juvenile 24/26 in.
  Tandems; Model H 28/30 in: Model I 28/18 in.
  Tricycles; 26/26 in.

1896: Safeties; Gent's Model B28/30 in: Others; 28/28 in or 28/30 in.
    Ladies' Beeston or Wolverhampton models 28/28 in with 26/28 in option.
    Coventry 26/28 in.
  Spring frame Safeties; 28/28 in or 28/30 in.
  Tandems; Model I 28/22 in: No. 17 28/28 in.
  Tricycles; Coventry 26/26 in: Roadster 26/28 in: Beeston 26/26 in.

1897: Gents' Safeties; 28/28 in (28/30 in option).
  Ladies' Safeties; 26/26 in: Models 11 & 12 26/28 in.
  Tricycles; 26/26 in.
  Youths' & Girls' Safeties; 26/26 in.
  Tandems; 28/28 in: Model I 28/22 in.

1898: Safeties; 28/28 in (28/30 in option).
  Youths' & Girls'; 26/26 in.
  Tricycles; Beeston: 26/26 in. Coventry Models F & G: 26/28 in.
  Tandems; Beeston No. 17 28/28 in: Coventry Model H 28/28 in: Coventry Model I 28/22 in.

Thereafter, adult machines were standardized as 28/28 in for Safeties and Tandems; Beeston tricycles at 26/26 in; Boys' & Girls' at 24/24 in. The 30 in front wheel option was still available as late as 1904.

(F) STANDARD FRAME SIZES

1897:	*Gents'*	*Ladies'*
	22 in	20 in
	24 in	22 in
	26 in	24 in

1898: As above plus:

			Front	Rear
Tandems:	Beeston Nos. 15 & 16;		22 in	21 in
			24 in	23 in
			26 in	25 in
	Coventry Model H (two Gents);		22 in	21 in
			24 in	23 in
			26 in	25 in
	Coventry Model H (Combination);		18 in	21 in
			20 in	23 in
			22 in	25 in
	Coventry Model I;		20 in	22 in
			22 in	24 in
			24 in	26 in

Juvenile Safeties: Model E; 18½ in
Model J; 16½ in

1900: Safeties:

Gents'	Ladies'
23 in	21 in
26 in	23 in
27 in	25 in

except Nos. 3, 7 & 15 which are 1 in lower

Juveniles: As 1898

Tandems:		Front	Rear
	No. 17	24 in	23 in
	No. 21	24 in	22 in

The above measurements are for the middle size, with ±2 in for larger or smaller sizes.
The adult frame sizes given for 1900 became standard thereafter.

Transfers

The trade mark transfer of the type appropriate to the model and the current company title appeared in the following positions on the machines:
(a)   On the centre line of the steering head pillar.
(b)   On the centre line of the rear mudguard (on those machines fitted with mudguards) just above the rear mudguard stay attachment.
The patterns of transfers used are shown in the illustrations (A and B). On Beeston Humber machines the head transfer took the form shown in (C) from 1901 and thereafter.
   Transfers other than those of the trade mark pattern appeared on the gearcases of machines fitted with these as follows:

Pre-1907: Pattern illustrated as (D). On machines fitted with leather gearcases this design was applied to the leather.
1907: Beeston Humber models with gearcases had 'Humber Ltd.' in cursive script applied centrally *below* the level of the chainstay.
1908: This design was applied to Beeston and Standard Special models.
1909–14: Applied to all models with metal gearcases. Leather or leather/celluloid gearcases did not carry this.
Post-war: All models with metal gearcases carried 'Humber Ltd'. in cursive script as pre-war, but the Royal Warrant Coat-of-Arms was superimposed centrally above the 'Humber Ltd'. (E)

Since the majority of surviving machines are likely to come from the 1890s onwards it is important to note the fact that the transfer designs applied to the machines carried the individual wording applicable to the factory of origin, i.e. Beeston, Wolverhampton or Coventry, as shown in the illustrations, and *not* the combined wording that appeared under the trade mark design in, for example, many catalogues and other publicity material. It is important, too, that the details of the wording that changed when the company underwent a change of title in 1900 from 'Humber & Co. Ltd.' to 'Humber Ltd.' should be noted. Unfortunately, it has not been possible to establish any precise date when the change in wording of the transfers took place, and it is in any case likely that old stocks were used up. However, the trade mark designs shown in the catalogues may serve as a fairly reliable guide. The catalogue issued for the year 1900 still carried the old wording 'Humber & Co. Ltd.' whereas that for 1901 bore the new wording 'Humber Ltd'. It would probably be correct to assume that any machine turned out in the first part of 1900 would have carried the earlier form of transfer and that from June or July 1900 the new pattern was introduced, remembering that the 1901 'season' began at the time of the big shows in the late autumn of 1900.

Frame Numbers

These were stamped in the following positions:

(i)   On the lower part of the steering head just above the fork crown. Above the frame number, details of the model designation.
(ii) On the lower part of the *near* side seat stay, immediately above the bolt hole affixing the stay to the chainstay and wheel spindle.
(iii) On the lower part of the handlebar stem. (This cannot be seen unless the handlebar is taken out complete.)

In the 1896 period frame numbers were stamped in the following additional positions:

(i)   On the underside of the downtube lug of the bottom bracket.
(ii)   Under the front fork crown.
(iii) On the front fork stem.
(iv)   On the handlebar lug.
(v)   On the headclamp.
(vi)   On the front axle.
(vii) On the rear mudguard at the chainstay end.

Finishing, Painting and Lining

As was commonplace, the majority of machines were turned out in black enamel, though there were recognized catalogued exceptions. The normal finish for aluminium-framed machines was the natural aluminium, though these could be had in black finish as an option. Full details of the painting and lining of the various models over the years are too complex to include here. Coloured finishes in lieu of black were a catalogued option at extra cost, as was the option of different standards or patterns of lining or different colours of lining. All-black finish with no plated parts became an option a few years prior to 1914. This option was followed by an alternative option of 'All-Stone-Grey' on certain models in 1914, but the latter was not continued after the First World War.

The Boudard Gear and the Simpson 'Lever' Chain

Humber 'wooed' both these short-lived devices, the Simpson Chain no doubt through the influence of E.T. Hooley who had a majority interest in the company that produced it and who was also at the time, much embroiled financially in Humber affairs. Both these devices were catalogued options on certain models in 1896, though it is certain that a fairly large number of machines fitted with the Boudard Gear were produced prior to this date.

Other 'Humbers'

Thomas Humber's apparent lack of care to protect the name of 'Humber' led to many copies of successful Humber designs, some of these even being named as 'Humber' machines. One such was the 'Humber' made by J.R. Whitehouse & Co., 52 Park Lane, Aston, Birmingham. It should also be made clear that the firm of Humber, Synyer & Co. Ltd., with registered offices at 5 Crocus Street, Nottingham, had no direct connection with Thomas

Humber of Beeston. Sam Humber, of Humber, Synyer, was a relative of Thomas Humber, but though the firm made cycles with a variety of names, it never made one simply called Humber. Likewise, the 'Humber' of the firm of Humber, Cripps & Goddard of Beeston, was one Frank Humber, son of Thomas Humber of Beeston, but again, the machines, known as 'Nelson' cycles, were not products of the genuine Humber factories with which this book is concerned.

Humber Transfer Designs

pre-1900

Beeston Make

Wolverhampton Make

Coventry Make

Obsolete Trade Mark
Used on Wolverhampton
and Coventry Machines only;
discontinued during 1897

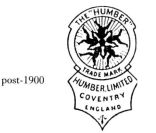

post-1900

post-1901

Abridged Details of Catalogued Models in Representative Years

YEAR	MODELS CATALOGUED	REMARKS
1873/4	1 Gents' basic model with options as to size	The 'Spider Bicycle' made in Nottingham. Driving wheel from 44 in to 50 in in 2 in steps. Finish enamelled or bright, with or without brake. 'V' tyres or steel optional. Prices from £12 to £14.
1878	1 Gents' basic model with options as to size	The Humber, built by Humber, Marriott & Cooper, Queen's Road, Nottingham. (The move to Beeston was made in the same year.) 44 in to 58 in driving wheel in 2 in steps. Prices from £13 5s. to £15. All high-quality machines.
1887	2 Ordinaries (Racer and Roadster) / 2 'Dwarf' Safeties; No. 1 Roadster / No. 2 Roadster / Tricycles; Gents' Cripper Roadster (Beeston) / Ladies' Cripper Tandem Roadster (Beeston)	The Safety bicycles sold at £20. The Beeston Humber Cripper tricycle cost £25, the Cripper Tandem £36. All high-quality machines.
1889	*Beeston-built:* / Ordinaries 3 / Gents' Safeties 5 / Tandem Safety 1 / Tricycles (2 Ladies' models) 5 / Tandem Tricycles 5 / *Wolverhampton/Coventry-built:* / Safeties 6 / Ordinaries (incl. 1 Juvenile) 5 / Tricycles (plus Ladies' model and 1 Carrier model) 4 / Juvenile Tandem Tricycle 1	A wide range of models and options. Prices ranged from £3 10s. for the smallest size of 'Wellington Junior Harrier' Tricycle to £34 for the Beeston Humber No. 1 Cripper Tandem.
1890	*Beeston built:* / Ordinaries 2 / Safeties 5 Gents', 1 Ladies' / Tricycles 3 Gents', 2 Ladies' / Tandem Tricycles 2 and a Tandem Attachment / *Wolverhampton/Coventry-built:* / Ordinaries 4 / Safeties 3 Gents' / Tricycles 3 Gents', 1 Ladies', 2 Juvenile (Coventry only) / 1 Box-Carrier (Wolverhampton only)	Pneumatic tyres an option on only one model Safety and one model each of Beeston Gents' and Ladies' Cripper tricycle, in all cases at extra cost. Patent 'Anti-Vibrator' and anti-vibration saddle pillar on some models. Direct spokes on all models. Plain bearings on some of the cheaper models. Diamond frames to all but one model of the Safeties. Slightly reduced range as compared with the previous year. Pneumatic tyre option the only innovation.

1892

Tandem Tricycles — 2 Juvenile

Beeston-built:
- Ordinaries — 2
- Safeties — 3 Gents'
- Tricycles — 1 Gents', 1 Ladies' (Gent's model with removable top tube)
- Tandem Tricycle — 1

Wolverhampton-built:
- Safeties — 3 Gents'
- Tandem Safety — 1 (*)

Coventry-built:
- Safeties — 2 Gents', 1 Ladies', 1 Military, 1 Youths', 1 Juvenile
- Tricycles — 1 (Ladies' or Gents'), 1 Juvenile, 1 Carrier, 1 Invalid Chair

The last year in which Ordinaries were catalogued. Pneumatic tyres at extra cost ranging from £3 10s. to £7 10s. Only one cross-frame Safety, all the rest diamond-frame. Beeston No. 1 Safety available with patent band brake on front wheel, in lieu of spoon brake, at extra cost of 10s. Coventry Roadster No. 11 had near side transmission. The Wolverhampton Tandem Safety had 'crossed' transmission, i.e. near side front chain, off side rear chain. The Carrier and Invalid Tricycles had a foot-operated spoon brake acting on the rear wheel. Prices from £6 for the smallest size Juvenile to £36 for the Beeston Tandem Tricycle. Pneumatic tyres an option on Ordinaries also.

1894

Beeston-built:
- All Safeties — 5 Gents', 1 Ladies'
- Tricycles — 3 Gents', 2 Ladies' (detachable top tube)
- Tandem Tricycle — 1

Wolverhampton/Coventry-built:
- Safeties — 3 Gents', 1 Ladies'
- Tandem Safety — 1

Prices ranged from £18 to £37, excluding cost of tyres. Humber Patent Semi-Tangent driving wheel fitted to some models in this year. Trotting Sulky catalogued.

1895

- Safeties — 3 Gents', 3 Ladies'
- Tandems — 3
- Tricycles — 2

These items probably refer only to Wolverhampton/Coventry-built machines. Although there is no indication of such, it would seem that this catalogue does not list Beeston-built machines, as all the previous year's catalogued Beeston models are not featured. Better quality models had tangent spokes to both wheels, cheaper quality had direct (radial) spokes. No mention of the semi-tangent wheel offered in the previous season. Trotting Sulky again listed.

1896

Beeston-built:
- Gents' Safeties — 4
- Ladies' " — 4
- Tricycles " — 3 (Ladies' detachable top tube option)
- Tandems " — 3 (1 being C.W. Brown's 'Self-Locking' frame)
- Triplet " — 1

Price range £10 to £45. Prices exclude cost of tyres (pneumatic). Innovations included the Spring Frame Safeties and C.W. Brown's Patent 'Self-Locking' triangulated frame for a Ladies' Safety and for a Tandem. Boudard Gear and Simpson 'Lever' Chain offered as extra on some models. Ladies' Safety frames included single-tube, dropped top tube, straight tubed and 'Self-Locking' types.

YEAR	MODELS CATALOGUED		REMARKS
	Wolverhampton-built:		
	Gents' Safeties	4	
	Ladies' "	4	
	Coventry built:		
	Gents' Safeties	3 (1 Spring frame model)	
	Ladies' "	4 (1 Spring frame model; 1 'Self-Locking' frame model)	
	Tricycles "	2	
	Tandem "	1 (Open front Model I)	
1897	*Beeston-built:*		Duplex chainstay on driving side on Beeston models (as introduced at the 1896 shows) and on Wolverhampton models. Patent band brake on extra on Nos. 1 & 2 Gents' Safeties, at extra cost. The old open-front Coventry-built Tandem Model I was dropped for this season.
	Gents' Safeties	4	
	Ladies' "	1	
	Tandems	3	
	Tricycles	4	
	Wolverhampton-built:		
	Gents' Safeties	4	
	Ladies' "	1	
	Coventry-built:		
	Safeties	1 Gents', 2 Ladies', 1 Youths, 1 Girls'	
1898	*Beeston-built:*		Innovations for the season included the 'Chainless' built under Acatène License and the Pedersen 'Cantilever', also built under license. These were the most expensive machines of the range at £36. The old Coventry open-front Tandem Model I was back in the catalogue. Aluminium-framed models were exhibited at the 1897 Stanley Show, but not, apparently catalogued for 1898. ⅝ in pitch roller chains standard for all Beeston and Wolverhampton machines; Coventry machines had 1 in pitch block chains as standard.
	Gents' Safeties	4	
	Ladies' "	1	
	Tandems	3	
	Tricycles	3	
	'Chainless' Safety	1 (with 4 Gents' detail options and 1 Lady's frame model)	
	Pedersen 'Cantilever'	1	
	Wolverhampton-built		
	Gents' Safeties	4	
	Ladies' "	1	
	Coventry-built:		
	Gents' Safeties	2	
	Ladies' "	1	
	Youths' "	1	
	Girls' "	1	
	Tricycles	2	

The Wolverhampton machines were now termed 'First Grade'. Number of models quoted includes Ladies' and Gents' machines. Beeston machines included three tricycle options and two tandem options. Free-wheel (termed 'Free Pedals') machines introduced. Rim brakes introduced. Aluminium models catalogued. Twenty-two models in the range with $5/8$ in pitch roller chain, six with 1 in pitch block chain and two with 1 in pitch double roller chain. Duplex front fork introduced on Beeston models.

Aluminium models offered. Beeston range included three tricycle options and three Tandem options. $5/8$ in pitch roller chain standard on all models of the entire range. Brakes generally improved with the spread of free-wheel models. 'Brazeless' (jointed) frames introduced at the 1897 shows mentioned only in passing in the introduction to catalogue. Part of the specification only on aluminium-framed machines.

A year in which the variety of options was impressive, including choice of diamond or duplex cross-frames on some Beeston and 1st-Grade models, aluminium framed Gents' models and spring-framed Gent's models. Minor options chiefly related to choices of gear (fixed or free-wheel) and of brakes. In the latter the system was that fixed wheel machines had front rim brake only as standard, with option of front and rear rim brakes or front rim and rear band brake on free-wheel machines. Road and path racers still brakeless. With all possible options included the range gave some fifty-four models, an extent never again offered in subsequent years. Prices for single safety machines ranged from 10 guineas to £25.

1900
- Tandems: 3
- *Beeston-built*: 14
- *Wolverhampton-built*: 7
- *Coventry-built*: 8

1901
- *Beeston-built*: 8 Gents', 3 Ladies'
- *1st-Grade (Coventry-built)*: 5 Gents', 3 Ladies'
- *'Standard' (Coventry-built)*: 6 Gents', 4 Ladies'

1902
- *Beeston-built*:
  - Gents': 5 basic models with 12 options
  - Ladies': 2 basic models with 7 options
- *1st-Grade (Beeston-built)*
  - Gents': 3 basic models with 8 options
  - Ladies': 2 basic models with 7 options
- *Beeston-built*
  - Tandems: 1 model with 3 options
  - Tricycles: 1 model with 3 options
- *Coventry-built*:
  - Standard Special: Gents': 1 model with 5 options
  - Ladies': 1 model with 3 options
  - Standard: Gents': 1 model with 3 options
  - Ladies': 1 model with 3 options

1903
- *Beeston-built*:
  - Gents': 4 basic with 1 option, plus 2 options of patent Duplex cross-frame to order
  - Ladies': 2 basic (1 with curved duplex cross frame) plus 1 option
  - Tandems: 3 models (Path Racer, Light Roadster, Combination Roadster)

YEAR	MODELS CATALOGUED		REMARKS
	Tricycles	1 basic, 2 options	Including all options the range in this year embraced thirty-four models as compared with the fifty-four offered in the previous season. The options offered a still wider choice of brakes.
	1st-Grade		
	Gents'	3 basic plus 1 option of duplex cross-frame on 2 models at no extra cost	
	Ladies'	2 basic (duplex curved cross-frame) with 1 option and 1 single curved frame	
	Standard Special		
	Gents'	2 basic plus 1 option	
	Ladies'	1 basic plus 1 option	
	Standard		
	Gents'	1 basic plus 2 options	
	Ladies'	1 basic plus 2 options	
1904	*Beeston-built:*		A much reduced range. Prices from 10 guineas to £22 10s. with the Beeston tricycle at £32. Two-speed hub gears* available at extra cost. 30 in front wheel still an optional extra. All models except the 'Standard' now had roller lever rim brakes or lever front and back-pedal band brake. 'Standard' models retained the inverted lever cable operated rim brakes. Beeston 'Aluminium' model still available. Beeston Road and Path Racers retained the duplex chainstay on the driven side, the only Beeston models to do so. Duplex cross-frame machines no longer catalogued, but an available option at no extra cost on Beeston or 1st-Grade Gents' machines.
	Gents'	3 basic models with 1 option	
	Ladies'	2 basic models with 1 option	
	Tricycles	1 basic model with 3 options	
	1st-Grade (*Beeston-built*):		
	Gents'	1 basic model with 3 options	
	Ladies'	2 basic models with 1 option	
	Coventry-built:		
	Gents'	3 models with 1 option	
	Ladies'	3 models with 1 option	
1905	*Beeston-built:*	6 models	Most expensive at 18 guineas, least expensive at 7 guineas. Roller lever rim brakes almost universal this season. Aluminium model still listed. Two-speed hub gear option available on many models. The only year in which the aluminium model (No. 2) was offered with 26 in wheels to low frames and 28 in to medium or high frames.
	Coventry-built:	8 models	
1906	Twenty-one models offered ranging in price from 7 guineas to 19 guineas. Aluminium model catalogued.		Beeston Lady's Duplex (curved) pattern introduced. Humber-Cordner three-speed hub gear introduced. Tandem and tricycle models available but not catalogued.
1907	Nineteen models catalogued, ranging in price from 6 guineas to £32 for the tricycle.		Aluminium model catalogued. Humber-Cordner gear now wire and pulley operated. No two-speed options listed.
1908	Twenty-one models catalogued from 5 guineas to £30 (tricycle).		Aluminium model catalogued. Humber-Cordner gear now in revised form, still wire and pulley operated. Humber-Cordner three-speed hub available on tricycles for the first time. Juvenile frame sizes 16 in or 18 in to order. Front rim brake standard

Year	Description	Models
1909	on Beeston tricycle as well as the long-established band brake on main axle. Beeston models now reduced to one basic plus one option each for Ladies' or Gents'. Beeston tricycle discontinued except to special order. Coventry tricycles with two-speed as standard, single-speed at option. Juvenile frame sizes altered to 17 in or 19 in to order. Sturmey-Archer hub three-speed gears replaced the Humber-Cordner.	Twenty one models catalogued, from 5 guineas to £23 (Coventry tricycles).
1910	Options as 1909 but two options on Club Road Racer, a 'bridge' between what was offered in this model in 1909 and what was to come in 1911. Two-speed gear standard on tricycles, as 1909. Beeston models increased in price from £14 in 1909 to 15 guineas.	Twenty-two models listed, from 5 guineas to £25 (tricycle).
1911	Two- and three-speed hub gears as option throughout the range. 'All-black' finish now an option on some models. Front mudguard extension standard on all the range except the 'Popular' and Juvenile models.	Twenty-two models listed from 5 guineas to £25 (tricycle).
1913	Beeston model one basic with one option for both Ladies' and Gents'.	Twenty models listed, from 5 guineas to £15 12s. 6d.
1914	'All-stone-grey' finish as an option to 'All-black' now available on some models. Beeston models as 1913.	Twenty models listed, from £4 10s to £15 12s. 6d.
1915	As 1914, with the addition of 'The Military Humber', equipped with back and front carriers, gun clips, lamp, bell and 'reflex' light at 9 guineas. All prices increased by 20 per cent 'due to increased costs of materials and labour'.	
1920	Variable gears available, options throughout the range. Prices raised on 1 May 1920 to £12 15s. to £24. 'Olympia' models the cheapest of the range.	Ten models offered, only one Lady's or Gents' Beeston model.
1921	'Olympia' models as before.	Ten models offered, options and prices as 1920 (revised prices).
1923	A Light Roadster (Gents'), cross-frame (single-tubed) (Gents') and Tradesman's. Carrier models were the additions to the previous range. 'All-black' finish optional on all models. 'Olympia' models the cheap end of the range still.	Thirteen models offered. Prices from 7 guineas to £18 7s.
1925	Cross-frame model still listed. Gents' 'Popular Tourist' and Gents' Road Racer additions to the range.	Sixteen models listed. Prices from £6 7s. 6d. to 15 guineas.
1929	'Club' racer model (Gents' only). 'Cob' models (26 in wheels, lower and smaller frames) an option to several models. Also 'All Weather' and 'Sports' options for Ladies' and Gents' machines. 'Olympia' models still the cheap end of the range.	Thirty-three models listed, including all options, prices from £5 12s. 6d. to £15 4s. 0d.

* Fagan two-speed gears.

Appendix III : Motor Cycles

YEAR	MODEL	NO. OF CYLINDERS	BORE AND STROKE	COOLING	DRIVE	PRICE	REMARKS
1896	2 hp Tandem Safety	2					Bicycle fitted with a Kane Pennington motor
1898	1½ hp Ladies' Motor Safety	1		Air	Belt	POA	Engine mounted behind the saddle and within the wheelbase
	2½ hp Combination Motor Tandem	2		Air	Direct	POA	Engine mounted on either side of rear wheel
	Léon-Bollée-type Forecar	1		"	Belt	POA	Fitted with pedals and electric motor for cycle pacing
	Electric Motor Tandem	1		"	Chain	POA	De-Dion-type tricycle
1899	1¾ hp	1		"	"	£114	As 1898
	Electric Tandem	1		"	"	£180	Engine mounted on outrigger behind rear wheel
	1¾ hp Olympia Tandem	1		"	"	£100	Side-by-side seating, tiller steering
	Léon-Bollée-type Motor Sociable	1		"	Belt	£170	
	2⅛ hp Léon-Bollée-type Forecar					£150	Single driver's seat with one or two passengers' seats forward
1902	1½ hp	1	2⅝ in × 3 in	Air	Belt	£45	Beeston model £55. Minerva-type
	2 hp	1	"	"	Chain	£50	Beeston model £60. Built under P & M licence
1903	1¾ hp	1	70 mm × 70 mm	"	"	£50	Beeston £60 "
	2¾ hp	1	76 mm × 76 mm	"	"	£55	Beeston £65 "
	2¾ hp Tricycle	1	" "	"	"	£65	Beeston £75 "
	2¾ hp Olympia Tandem	1	" "	"	"	75 guineas	Beeston 85 guineas "
1904	2 hp	1	70 mm × 70 mm	Air	Chain	£42	Beeston £50 "
	2¾ hp	1	76 mm × 76 mm	"	"	£45	Beeston £55 "
	3½ hp Olympia Tandem	1	89 mm × 101 mm	Water	"	£85	Beeston £90, two speeds
1905	1¾ hp	1	65 mm × 76 mm	Air	"	£40	"
	3 hp	1		Water	"	£43	Free-engine clutch £2 10s. extra
	4½ hp Olympia Tandem	1		Water	"	£85	Two speeds "
	5 hp Olympia Tricar	1			"	£95	Two speeds, wheel steering "
1909	3½ hp	1	83 mm × 90 mm	Air	Belt	£45	Two speeds "
1910	2 hp	1	60 mm × 70 mm	"	"	£37	
	3½ hp	1	83 mm × 90 mm	"	"	£45	With two-speed gear £50
1911	2 hp	1	60 mm × 70 mm	"	"	£37	
	3½ hp	1	83 mm × 90 mm	"	"	£45	Single speed and pedal gear. With two-speed Roc gear in rear hub £50

Year / Model	Cylinders	Bore × Stroke	Cooling	Drive	Price	Notes
1912 2 hp	1	60 mm × 70 mm	"	"	£35	Free-engine hub £4 extra. Three-speed hub gear £10 10s. extra
2¾ hp TT	2 V-twin	60 mm × 60 mm	"	"	£42	Extras as above
3½ hp	1	84 mm × 90 mm	"	"	£47 10s.	Free-engine hub £4 extra. Two-speed Roc gear complete at £52 10s. Sidecars listed at £10 17s. 6d.
1913 2 hp	1	60 mm × 70 mm	"	"	£35	Three-speed Armstrong gear £10 10s. extra
2¾ hp TT	2 V-twin	60 mm × 60 mm	"	"	£43 10s.	Three-speed Armstrong hub gear standard
3½ hp	1	84 mm × 90 mm	"	"	£57 10s.	Three-speed Sturmey-Archer gear standard
1914 2 hp	1	60 mm × 70 mm	"	"	£35	Armstrong three-speed hub gear £10 10s. extra
2¾ hp TT	2 V-twin	60.75 mm × 60 mm	"	"	£52 10s.	Three-speed Sturmey-Archer gear standard
3½ hp	1	84 mm × 90 mm	Water	"	£52 10s.	Three-speed Sturmey-Archer gear standard
1915 3½ hp	1	84 mm × 90 mm	Air	"	£63	Three-speed Sturmey-Archer gear standard
6 hp	1	84 mm × 90 mm	Water	"	£57 10s.	Three-speed countershaft gearbox. With sidecar £98
1916 3½ hp	2 Flat-twin	78 mm × 78 mm	Water	Chain	£85	Three-speed countershaft gearbox
6 hp	2 Flat-twin	68 mm × 68.75 mm	Air	"	£75	Three-speed countershaft gearbox. With sidecar £104
1917 All as 1916						
1918 All as 1917						
1919 3½ hp model only	2 Flat-twin	78 mm × 78 mm	Water	"	£89 5s.	
1920 3½ hp	2 Flat-twin	68 mm × 68.75 mm	Water	Chain	£125 solo	Combination £150 5s.
4½ hp	2 Flat-twin	75 mm × 68 mm	Air	"	£130 solo	Combination £155 5s.
1921 4½ hp	2 Flat-twin	75 mm × 68 mm	Air	"	£140 solo	Combination £173 12s. 6d. Sports model £140
1922 4½ hp	2 Flat-twin	"	"	"	£110 solo	Combination £144. Sports model £100 solo
1923 2¾ hp lightweight	1	75 mm × 79 mm	"	"	£65	Three-speed countershaft gearbox
4½ hp	2 Flat-twin	75 mm × 68 mm	"	"	£99 solo	Combination £120 10s. Sports model solo £89
1924 2¾ hp lightweight	1	75 mm × 79 mm	"	"	£55 solo	Combination £105
1925 2¾ hp lightweight	1	"	"	"	£50 sports	Sports model. Touring model £55 7s. 6d.
1926 2¾ hp De Luxe	1	"	"	"	£46 10s.	Solo. Touring model £50 7s. 6d. 'Six Days' model £47 10s. Sports, £47 17s. 6d. touring. Sidecars at £15 15s.
1927 3.49 hp	1	"	"	"	"	Side-valve touring. Sports model ohv £51 10s. Sidecars listed at £15 15s.
1928 3.49 hp	1	"	"	"	"	Side-valve touring. Sports model ohv £51 10s. Over-head camshaft Sports £60 to £63. Sidecars at £16 10s.
1929 3.49 hp	All as 1928				sv £45	ohv £48 10s. ohc £59 10s.
1930 3.49 hp	All as 1929				sv £44 10s.	ohv £48. ohc £56. Sidecars at £16 10s.

Appendix IV : Motor Cars

1900–15

YEAR	MODEL	NO. OF CYLINDERS	BORE/STROKE (IN) CAPACITY (CC)	CARBURETTOR	VALVES	IGNITION	LUBRICATION	TRANSMISSION (B)–BEVEL, (W)–WORM	NO. OF SPEEDS	CHASSIS FRAME	WHEELS	WHEELBASE	TRACK	REMARKS
1900	3½ hp Phaeton	1 h							2	s/t				Front wheel drive, rear wheel steering.
	5 hp Phaeton	1 h							4	s/t				
	2¾ hp M.D. Voiturette	1 h							2	s/t				
1901	4½ hp	1 v		De-Dion		C		c/c l/a B	2	s/t	Wi			De-Dion engine. First model with single-spoke steering wheel.
1902	8 hp	2 v	3½ × 4 1261		side exh. AI	C	sight feed & splash	c/c l/a B		s/t				
	9½ hp	2 v	4 × 4½ 1853					c/c l/a B	3		A			
	12 hp	4 vp	3½ × 4 2523		side exh. AI	C	sight feed & splash		4		A	7 ft 0 in	4 ft 3 in	
1903	5 hp Coventry & Beeston Humberette	1 v	3⅝ × 3⅝ 613	Longuemare	side exh. AI	C	sight feed & splash	c/c l/a B	2	s/t	Wi	5 ft 3 in	3 ft 6 in	
	12 hp Beeston	4 vp	3⅝ × 4 2706	Longuemare	side	C	sight feed & splash	c/c l/a B	4	s/t	A	8 ft 6 in	4 ft 3 in	
	20 hp Beeston	4 vp	4¼ × 5¾ 5347	"	T-head	"	"	"	4	"	"	9 ft 6 in	4 ft 3 in	
1904	5 hp Coventry & Beeston Humberette	1 v	3⅝ × 4 677	"	side exh. AI	C	"	"	2	"	Wi A	5 ft 3 in	3 ft 6 in	
	6½ hp Coventry & Beeston Royal Humberette	1 v	3⅞ × 4 773	"	"	C	"	"	3	"	A	5 ft 3 in	3 ft 6 in	August 1904 bore/stroke increased to 4" × 4½".
	8½ hp	2 v	3⅝ × 4¼ 1437	"	"		"	"	3	"	A	6 ft 4 in	3 ft 10 in	
	14 hp	4 vp	3⅝ × 4 2706		side	C	"	"	4	"	A	8 ft 6 in	4 ft 3 in	
	25 hp	4 vp	4 × 4¼ 3707		T-head	"	"	"	4	"	A	9 ft 6 in	4 ft 3 in	
1905	5 hp Coventry & Beeston	1 v	3⅝ × 4 677	Longuemare	side exh. AI	C	"	"	2	"	Wi	5 ft 3 in	3 ft 6 in	

	Humberette 6½ hp Royal Humberette	1 v	3⅞ × 4 773	"	"	C	"	"	3	"	A	5 ft 3 in	3 ft 6 in	
	7½ hp Beeston Royal Humberette	2 v	3½ × 4½ 1419	"	side T-head	C	"	"	3	"	A	6 ft 6 in	4 ft 3 in	
	8/10 hp Coventry	4 sv	3⅛ × 3¾ 1885	Longuemare	side	C	"	"	3	"	"	6 ft 8 in	4 ft 0 in	
	8/10 hp Beeston	4s	77 mm x 108 m/m"			C	Sight feed & splash		3			6 ft 9 in	4 ft 1 in	
	10/12 hp	2 vp	4 × 4¼ 1751	"	side exh. AI	"	"	"	3	"	"	7 ft 6 in	3 ft 10 in	
	12/14 hp	4 vp	3⅝ × 4 2706	"	side T-head	"	"	"	4	"	"	8 ft 6 in	4 ft 3 in	
	20/25 hp	4 vp	4¼ × 5¾ 5347	"	"	"	"	"	4	"	"	9 ft 6 in	4 ft 3 in	
1906	10/12 hp Coventry	4 s	3½ × 3¾ 2365	Longuemare	side T-head	"	sight feed & pump	"	3	"	"	8 ft 0 in	4 ft 0 in	Short chassis 7 ft 1 in WB
	16/20 hp Beeston	4 s	95 mm × 125 mm 3544		"	"	pump & splash	"	4	psc	"	8 ft 6 in	4 ft 3 in	Engine increased later to 100 mm × 130 mm 4084 cc WB increased to 8 ft 10 in
1907	10/12 hp Coventry	4 s	3½ × 3¾ 2365	Not specified	side T-head	"	"	"	3	s/t	"	8 ft 0 in	4 ft 3 in	Short chassis 7 ft 1 in WB
	15 hp Coventry	4 s	3¾ × 4½ 3258	"	"	"	"	"	3	psc s/t sub-frame	"	8 ft 9 in	4 ft 3 in	
	30 hp Beeston	4 s	110 mm × 130 mm 4942	"	"	M & C	"	"	4	psc	"	9 ft 3 in	4 ft 4 in	Engine later increased to 120 mm × 140 mm 6333 cc
1908	10/12 hp Coventry	4 s	3¼ × 3¾ 2039	Longuemare	"	C	"	"	3	"	"	8 ft 0 in	4 ft 0 in	Short chassis 7 ft 1 in WB Cabs: track of 4 ft 7 in
	15 hp Coventry	4 s	3⅞ × 4½ 3479	"	"	"	"	"	3	"	"	8 ft 10 in	4 ft 3 in	
	20 hp Beeston	4 s	105 mm × 130 mm 4503	Automatic	"	M & C	"	"	4	"	"	9 ft 3 in	4 ft 6 in	
	30 hp Coventry	6 p	4 × 4½ 5560	"	"	"	"	"	3	"	"	9 ft 10 in	4 ft 4 in	
	30 hp Beeston	4 p	120 mm × 150 mm 6786	"	"	H/T & L/T M	"	"	4	"	"	10 ft 2 in	4 ft 6 in	
1909	8 hp	2 m	90 mm × 120 mm 1527	"	side L-head	M & C	pump	"	3	"	"	7 ft 6 in	4 ft 0 in	
	12 hp	4 p	90 mm × 95 mm 2417	"	side T-head	C	"	"	3	"	"	8 ft 0 in	4 ft 0 in	
	16 hp	4 s	100 mm × 130 mm 4084	"	"	"	"	"	4	"	"	9 ft 3 in	4 ft 6 in	
	20 hp	4 s	105 mm × 130 mm 4503	"	"	M & C	"	"	4	"	"	9 ft 3 in	4 ft 6 in	
	30 hp	6 p	102 mm × 114 mm 5589	"	"	M & C	"	"	4	"	"	9 ft 10 in	4 ft 4 in	
1910	8 hp	2 m	90 mm × 120 mm 1527	"	side L-head	M	"	"	3	"	AD	7 ft 6 in	4 ft 0 in	
	12 hp	4 p	90 mm × 100 mm 2545	Automatic	side T-head	M	"	"	4	"	AD	8 ft 9 in	4 ft 6 in	
	16 hp	4 p	100 mm × 130 mm 4084	"	"	M & C	"	"	4	"	"	9 ft 3 in	4 ft 6 in	LWB 10 ft 9 in

YEAR	MODEL	NO. OF CYLINDERS	BORE/STROKE (IN) / CAPACITY (CC)	CARBURETTOR	VALVES	IGNITION	LUBRICATION	TRANSMISSION BEVEL (B) – WORM (W)	NO. OF SPEEDS	CHASSIS FRAME	WHEELS	WHEELBASE	TRACK	REMARKS
1911	10/14 hp	4 p	76 mm × 110 mm 1996	"	"	M	"	"	4	"	Wi D	8 ft 10 in	4 ft 10 in	
	12/20 hp	4 p	90 mm × 100 mm 2545	"	"	"	"	"	4	"	"	9 ft 1½ in	4 ft 9 in	LWB 10 ft 1½ in
	16/24 hp	4 p	100 mm × 130 mm 4084	"	"	M & C	"	"	4	"	AD	9 ft 3 in	4 ft 10 in	LWB 10 ft 9 in
	28 hp	4 p	105 mm × 140 mm 4849	"	"	"	"	"	4	"	Wi D	9 ft 10½ in	4 ft 10 in	LWB 10 ft 10½ in
1912	11 hp	4 m	68 mm × 120 mm 1744	"	side L-head	M	"	"	3	"	Wi	8 ft 4 in	4 ft 2 in	Wheels non-detachable
	14 hp	4 p	78 mm × 110 mm 2103	"	"	"	"	c/c l/a W	3	"	Wi D	8 ft 10 in	4 ft 2 in	
	12–20 hp	4 p	90 mm × 100 mm 2546	"	side T-head	"	"	c/c l/a B	4	"	Wi D	9 ft 1½ in	4 ft 9 in	LWB 10 ft 1½ in
	20 hp	4 p	90 mm × 120 mm 3054	"	"	M & C	"	c/c l/a W	4	"	"	9 ft 4 in	4 ft 9 in	LWB 10 ft 4 in
	28 hp	4 p	105 mm × 140 mm 4849	"	"	"	"	c/c l/a B	4	"	"	9 ft 10 in	4 ft 10 in	LWB 10 ft 10 in
1913	Humberette	2	84 mm × 90 mm 998	"	side	M	sight feed & splash	"	3	s/t	Wi	7 ft 5 in	3 ft 6 in	V-twin, air-cooled
	11 hp	4 m	69 mm × 130 mm 1944	"	side L-head	"	pump	"	4	psc	Wi D	8 ft 11 in	4 ft 7 in	SWB 8 ft 4 in
	14 hp	4 m	75 mm × 130 mm 2297	"	"	"	"	"	4	"	"	9 ft 2 in	4 ft 7 in	
	20 hp	4 p	90 mm × 120 mm 3054	"	side	M & C	pump	c/c l/a W	4	psc	Wi D	9 ft 4 in	4 ft 9 in	LWB 10 ft 4 in
	28 hp	4 p	105 mm × 140 mm 4849	"	side T-head	"	"	c/c l/a B	4	"	"	9 ft 10 in	4 ft 10 in	LWB 10 ft 10 in
1914	Humberette	2	84 mm × 90 mm 998	Smiths	side	M	sight feed & splash	"	3	s/t	Wi	7 ft 5 in	3 ft 6 in	V-twin, air- or water-cooled
	10 hp	4 m	65 mm × 120 mm 1593	"	side L-head	"	pump, trough & splash	"	4	psc	AD	8 ft 9½ in	4 ft 7 in	Bolt-on steel artillery wheels introduced
	11 hp	4 m	69 mm × 130 mm 1944	"	"	"	pump	"	4	"	Wi D	8 ft 11 in	4 ft 7 in	SWB 8 ft 4 in
	14 hp	4 m	75 mm × 140 mm 2474	"	"	"	"	"	4	"	AD	9 ft 5 in	4 ft 9 in	
	20 hp	4 p	90 mm × 130 mm 3308	Automatic	"	M & C	"	c/c l/a W	4	"	Wi D	9 ft 4 in	4 ft 9 in	LWB 10 ft 4 in
	28 hp	4 p	105 mm × 140 mm 4849	"	side T-head	"	"	c/c l/a B	4	"	Wi D	10 ft 10 in	4 ft 10 in	LWB 10 ft 4 in
1915	Humberette	2	84 mm × 90 mm 998	Smiths	side	M	sight feed & splash	"	3	s/t	Wi	7 ft 5 in	3 ft 6 in	V-twin, water-cooled
	10 hp	4 m	65 mm × 120 mm 1593	"	side L-head	"	pump, trough & splash	"	4	psc	AD	8 ft 3 in	4 ft 1 in	LWB 8 ft 9½ in & track 4 ft 7 in

Year / Model	Cyl	Bore × Stroke / cc	Carburettor	Valve	M/C	Lubrication	c/c l/a B	No.	Cooling	Wheelbase	Track	Notes
11 hp	4 m	69 mm × 130 mm / 1944	"	"	"	pump	"	4	"	Wi D 8 ft 11 in	4 ft 7 in	SWB 8 ft 4 in
14 hp	4 m	75 mm × 140 mm / 2474	"	"	"	"	"	4	"	AD 9 ft 5 in	4 ft 9 in	

1919-32

Year	Model	Cyl	Bore × Stroke / cc	Carburettor	Valve	M/C	Lubrication	c/c l/a B	No.	Cooling	Wheelbase	Track	Notes
1919	10 hp	4m	65 × 120 / 1593	Smiths	side L-head	M	pump trough & splash	c/c l/a B	4	psc	AD 8 ft 3 in	4 ft 1½ in	Two-seater Four-seater had WB 8 ft 9½ in and track 4 ft 7 in
	14 hp	4m	75 × 140 / 2474	"	"	"	pump	"	4	"	9 ft 5 in	4 ft 9 in	Four-seater as 1919
1920	10 hp	4m	65 × 120 / 1593	"	"	"	pump trough & splash	"	4	"	8 ft 3 in	4 ft 1½ in	
	15.9 hp	4m	80 × 140 / 2815	"	"	"	pump	"	4	"	10 ft 3½ in	4 ft 9 in	
1921	10 hp	4m	68 × 120 / 1743	Cox-Atmos	"	"	pump trough & splash	"	4	"	8 ft 9½ in	4 ft 7 in	
	15.9 hp	4m	80 × 140 / 2815	"	"	"	pump	"	4	"	10 ft 3½ in	4 ft 9 in	
1922	11.4 hp	4m	68 × 120 / 1743	"	"	"	pump trough & splash	"	4	"	8 ft 9½ in	4 ft 7 in	
	15.9 hp	4m	80 × 140 / 2815	"	"	"	pump	"	4	"	10 ft 3½ in	4 ft 9 in	
1923	8 hp	4m	56 × 100 / 985	"	ioe	C	pump trough & splash	"	3	"	7 ft 10½ in	3 ft 10 in	
	11.4 hp	4m	68 × 120 / 1743	"	"	M	"	"	4	"	9 ft 1 in	4 ft 7 in	
	15.9 hp	4m	80 × 140 / 2815	"	"	"	pump	"	4	"	10 ft 3½ in	4 ft 9 in	
1924	8 hp	4m	56 × 100 / 985	"	"	"	pump trough & splash	"	3	"	7 ft 10½ in	3 ft 10 in	
	11.4 hp	4m	68 × 120 / 1743	"	"	"	"	"	4	"	9 ft 1 in	4 ft 7 in	
	15.9 hp	4m	80 × 140 / 2815	"	"	"	pump	"	4	"	10 ft 3½ in	4 ft 9 in	
1925	8/18 hp	4m	56 × 100 / 985	"	"	"	pump trough & splash	"	3	"	7 ft 10½ in	3 ft 10 in	
	12/25 hp	4m	69 × 120 / 1795	"	"	"	"	"	4	"	9 ft 1 in	4 ft 7 in	
	15/40 hp	4m	80 × 140 / 2815	"	"	"	pump	"	4	"	10 ft 3½ in	4 ft 9 in	
1926	9/20 hp	4m	58 × 100 / 1056	"	"	"	pump trough & splash	"	3	"	8 ft 6 in	4 ft 0⅜ in	
	12/25 hp	4m	69 × 120 / 1795	"	"	"	"	"	4	"	9 ft 1 in	4 ft 7½ in	
	15/40 hp	4m	80 × 140 / 2815	"	"	"	pump	"	4	"	10 ft 6 in	4 ft 9 in	
1927	9/20 hp	4m	58 × 100 / 1056	"	"	"	pump trough & splash	"	3	"	8 ft 6 in	4 ft 0⅜ in	

Year	Model	No. of Cylinders	Bore/Stroke (in) / Capacity (cc)	Carburettor	Valves	Ignition	Lubrication	Transmission (B) – Bevel (W) – Worm	No. of Speeds	Chassis Frame	Wheels	Wheelbase	Track	Remarks
1927	14/40 hp	4m	75 × 116 / 2050	"	"	"	"	"	4	"	"	9 ft 8 in	4 ft 8 in	
	15/40 hp	4m	80 × 140 / 2815	"	"	"	pump	"	4	"	"	10 ft 6 in	4 ft 9 in	
	20/55 hp	6m	75 × 116 / 3075	"	"	"	"	"	4	"	"	10 ft 6 in	4 ft 9 in	LWB 10 ft 9 in
1928	9/20 hp	4m	58 × 100 / 1056	"	"	"	pump trough & splash	plate clutch l/a B	3	"	"	8 ft 6 in	4 ft 0⅜ in	
	14/40 hp	4m	75 × 116 / 2050	"	"	"	pump	"	4	"	"	9 ft 8 in	4 ft 8 in	
	20/55 hp	6m	75 × 116 / 3075	"	"	"	"	"	4	"	"	10 ft 6 in	4 ft 9 in	LWB 10 ft 9 in
1929	9/28 hp	4m	58 × 100 / 1056	Zenith	"	C	"	"	3	"	"	8 ft 6 in	4 ft 0⅜ in	
	14/40 hp	4m	75 × 116 / 2050	"	"	M	"	"	4	"	"	9 ft 8 in	4 ft 8 in	
	16/50 hp	6m	65 × 106 / 2110	"	"	C	"	"	4	"	"	10 ft 2 in	4 ft 8 in	
	20/65 hp	6m	75 × 116 / 3075	"	"	M	"	"	4	"	"	11 ft 0 in	4 ft 9 in	
1930	9/28 hp	4m	58 × 100 / 1056	"	"	C	"	"	3	"	Wi D	8 ft 6 in	4 ft 0⅜ in	
	16/50 hp	6m	65 × 106 / 2110	Stromberg	"	"	"	"	4	"	"	10 ft 0 in	4 ft 8 in	
	20/65 hp	6m	75 × 116 / 3075	Zenith	"	M	"	"	4	"	AD	11 ft 0 in	4 ft 9 in	
	Snipe	6m	80 × 116 / 3498·5	Stromberg	"	C	"	"	4	"	Wi D	10 ft 0 in	4 ft 8 in	
1931	16/50 hp	6m	65 × 106 / 2110	"	"	"	"	"	4	"	"	10 ft 0 in	4 ft 8 in	
	Snipe	6m	80 × 116 / 3498·5	"	"	"	"	"	4	"	"	10 ft 0 in	4 ft 8 in	
	Pullman	6m	80 × 116 / 3498·5	"	"	"	"	"	4	"	"	11 ft 0 in	4 ft 9 in	Central gearchange and handbrake controls on all models
1932	16/50 hp	6m	65 × 106 / 2110	"	"	"	"	"	4	"	"	10 ft 0 in	4 ft 8 in	
	Snipe	6m	80 × 116 / 3498·5	"	"	"	"	"	4	"	"	10 ft 0 in	4 ft 8 in	
	Pullman	6m	80 × 116 / 3498·5	"	"	"	"	"	4	"	"	11 ft 0 in	4 ft 8 in	Central gear-change and handbrake controls on all models

GLOSSARY

A	Artillery	D	Detachable	LT	Low Tension	s	Separate
AI	Automatic inlet	h	Horizontal	M	Magneto	s/t	Steel tube
B	Bevel	HT	High Tension	m	Monobloc	v	Vertical
C	Coil ignition	ioe	Inlet overhead, side exhaust valves	p	Paired	W	Worm
c/c	Cone clutch	l/a	Live axle	psc	Pressed steel channel	Wi	Wire

156

Body Styles and Prices

YEAR	MODEL	BODY	SEATS	PRICE
1900	2¾ hp MD Voiturette	Open	2	
	3½ hp Phaeton	Open	2	
	5 hp Phaeton	Open	2	
1901	4½ hp	r/e tonneau	4	£275
		r/e tonneau dl	4	300 g.
1902	8 hp			
	9½ hp	Doctor's car hs	2	
	12 hp	Tonneau re	4	£700
1903	5 hp C Humberette	Open	2	£125
	5 hp B Humberette	Open	2	£150
	9 hp			
	12 hp Beeston	Tonneau re	4	550 g.
	20 hp Beeston	Tonneau re		750 g.
		RdB re		800 g.
1904	5 hp C Humberette	Open	2	125 g.
	5 hp B Humberette	Open	2	140 g.
	6½ hp CR Humberette	Open	2	150 g.
	6½ hp BR Humberette	Open	2	160 g.
	8½ hp		4	250 g.
	14 hp		4	575 g.
	25 hp		4	800 g.
1905	5 hp C Humberette	Open	2	125 g.
	5 hp B Humberette	Open	2	140 g.
	6½ hp CR Humberette	Open	2	150 g.
	6½ hp BR Humberette	Open	2	160 g.
	7½ hp BR Humberette	Open	2	200 g.
	8/10 hp Coventry	Open	2	225 g.
	8/10 hp Coventry	Phaeton	3	240 g.
	8/10 hp Coventry	Phaeton	4	255 g.
	10/12 hp Coventry	Phaeton se	4	385 g.
		Landaulette	4	385 g.
	12/14 hp Coventry	Tonneau	4	375 g.
		Double Phaeton se	4	385 g.
	20/25 hp	Tonneau	4	450 g.
		Double Phaeton se	4	460 g.
1906	10/12 hp Coventry	Open swb	2	£270
		Double Phaeton lwb	4	£315
		Double with cs	4	£345
		Landaulette	4	£415
	16/20 hp Beeston	RdB	4	£472 10s.
		RdB with cch	4	£492 10s.
		RdB with cs	4	£502 10s.
		Landaulette	4	£592 10s.
		Landaulette	6	£622 10s.
1907	10/12 hp Coventry	Open swb	2	£270
		Open hs	2	£290
		Double Phaeton	4	£315
		Double cch	4	£335
		Double cs	4	£345

YEAR	MODEL	BODY	SEATS	PRICE
	10/12 hp Coventry	Special TT model		£800
	15 hp Coventry	RdB	4	£340
		RdB with cch	4	£355
		RdB with cs	4	£365
		Landaulette		£435
		Berline		£485
		Limousine		£455
	30 hp Beeston	RdB	5	£525
		RdB with hs	5	£563 13s.
		RdB with cs	5	£560
		Landaulette	6	£675
		Special TT model		£495
		Limousine/Berline	6	£675
1908	10/12 hp Coventry	Open	2	£235
		Open	4	£250
		Doctor's Car	2	£270
		Two-seat Motor Cab	4	£300
		Four-seat Motor Cab	5	£350
	15 hp Coventry	RdB	4	£315
		RdB with cch	4	£330
		RdB with cs	4	£345
		Landaulette	4	£415
		Landaulette with es	4	£435
		Limousine with cs	4	£465
	20 hp Beeston	RdB	4	£425
		RdB with cch	4	£450
		RdB with hs	4	£462
		RdB with cs	4	£465
		Limousine with cs	4	£550
		Limousine with cs	6	£575
		Landaulette with cs	4	£550
		Landaulette with D-front	6	£595
		Landaulette to form open carriage	6	£585
	30 hp Coventry	Standard body	5	£450
		Standard with cch	5	£465
		Standard with cs	5	£480
		Limousine with cs	4	£570
		Limousine with cs	6	£600
		Landaulette	6	£550
		Landaulette with es	6	£570
	30 hp Beeston	RdB	5	£575
		RdB with hs	5	£612
		RdB with cs	5	£615
		Limousine or Berline with cs	4	£700
		Limousine or Berline with cs	6	£725
		Landaulette with cs	4	£700
		Landaulette with cs	6	£725
		Landaulette with D-front	6	£745
		Landaulette to form open carriage	6	£735
1909	8 hp	Open	2	£195
	12 hp	Open	2	£235
		Double Phaeton	4	£250
		Doctor's car	2	£270

YEAR	MODEL	BODY	SEATS	PRICE
		Doctor's Landaulette	4	£330
		Doctor's Landaulette with e	4	£337 10s.
		Doctor's Landaulette with es	4	£342 10s.
		Traveller's car	3 & shelves	£350
		Motor cab	4	£325
		Motor cab with e	4	£332 10s.
		Motor cab with es	4	£337 10s.
	16 hp	Double Phaeton	5	£385
		Double with cch	5	£405
		Double with cs	5	£415
		Limousine with cs	4	£510
		Limousine with cs	6	£535
		Landaulette	4	£485
		Landaulette	6	£510
	20 hp	Open	5	£410
		Open with cch	5	£430
		Open with cs	5	£440
		Limousine with cs	4	£535
		Limousine with cs	6	£560
		Landaulette with cs	4	£535
		Landaulette with cs	6	£560
		Landaulette to form open carriage	6	£570
		Landaulette with D-front	6	£580
	30 hp	RdB	5	£495
		RdB with cch	5	£515
		RdB with cs	5	£525
		Landaulette with cs	4	£620
		Landaulette with cs	6	£645
		Limousine with cs	4	£595
		Limousine with cs	6	£620
1910	8 hp	Open	2	£200
	12 hp	Open	2	£270
		Racing Type	2	£285
		Doctor's Car	2	£305
		Double Phaeton	4	£285
		Limousine	4	£385
		Landaulette	4	£385
	16 hp	Open	2	£410
		RdB	5	£425
		RdB with hs	5	£453 8s.
		Limousine with cs	4	£565
		Limousine with cs	6	£590
		Landaulette	4	£540
		Landaulette with cs	6	£590
1911	10/14 hp	Open	2	£295
	12/20 hp	Open	2	£330
		Torpedo	4	£345
		Landaulette	4	£445
		Grafton Landaulette	6	£505
	16/24 hp	Open	2	£405
		Torpedo	4	£425
		Grafton Landaulette	6	£460
	28 hp	Open	2	£465

YEAR	MODEL	BODY	SEATS	PRICE
		Double Phaeton Rotund	4	£490
		Grafton Limousine with cs	4	£650
		Limousine with cs	6	£655
		Landaulette with cs	6	£655
		Grafton Landaulette with cs	6	£700
1912	11 hp	Open	2	£270
		Torpedo	4	£285
		Coupé Limousine	2	£370
		Coupé Landaulette	2	£370
	14 hp	Open	2	£295
		Torpedo	4	£310
		Coupé Limousine	2	£395
		Coupé Landaulette	2	£395
	12/20 hp	Open	2	£330
		Torpedo	4	£345
		Torpedo with hs	4	£370
	20 hp	Open	2	£370
		Torpedo	5	£385
		Landaulette	4	£500
		Landaulette	6	£550
		Cabrio-Phaeton	6	£550
		Cabriolet	6	£585
		Limousine	6	£550
		Grafton Landaulette	6	£605
		Pullman Limousine	6	£650
	28 hp	Open	2	£465
		Double Phaeton Rotund	5	£490
		Landaulette	4	£605
		Landaulette	6	£655
		Cabrio-Phaeton	6	£655
		Cabriolet	6	£690
		Limousine	6	£655
		Grafton Landaulette	6	£710
		Pullman Limousine	6	£755
1913	Humberette	Open	2	£115
		Open with hs and lights	2	£125
	11 hp	Open	2	£280
		Open with hs and lights	2	£295
		Torpedo	4	£295
		Torpedo with hs and lights	4	£310
		Coupé Landaulette	2	£395
	14 hp	Open with hs and lights	2	£340
		Torpedo	4	£355
		Landaulette	4	£480
		Limousine	4	£480
		Coupé Landaulette	2	£440
	20 hp	Open with hs	2	£430
		Torpedo	5	£445
		Cabrio-Phaeton	6	£570
		Cabriolet	6	£580
		Landaulette	6	£580
		Limousine	6	£580

YEAR	MODEL	BODY	SEATS	PRICE
	28 hp	Open	2	£490
		Double Phaeton Rotund	5	£515
		Cabrio-Phaeton	6	£640
		Cabriolet	6	£650
		Landaulette	6	£650
		Limousine	6	£650
1914	Humberette	Open (air-cooled engine with hs)	2	£120
		Open (water-cooled) with hs	2	£135
	10 hp	Open with hs and lights	2	£255
		Torpedo with hs and lights	4	£270
	11 hp	Open	2	£275
		Open with hs, lights, swt	2	£295
		Torpedo	4	£290
		Torpedo with hs, lights, swt	4	£310
	14 hp	Open with hs, swt, els	2	£380
		Torpedo with hs, swt, els	5	£395
		Coupé Landaulette with hs, swt, els	2	£480
		Landaulette with hs, swt, els	4	£520
	20 hp	Open with hs, lights, swt	2	£430
		Torpedo with hs, lights, swt	5	£445
		Cabrio-Phaeton	6	£570
		Cabriolet	6	£580
		Cabriolet de luxe	6	£625
		Landaulette	6	£580
		Limousine	6	£580
	28 hp	Double Phaeton Rotund	5	£470
		Cabrio-Phaeton	6	£595
		Cabriolet	6	£605
		Cabriolet de Luxe	6	£650
		Landaulette	6	£605
		Limousine	6	£605
1915	Humberette	Open, water-cooled engine, with hs and lights	2	£135
	10 hp	Open, hs, els	2–3	£280
		Torpedo with hs, els	4	£310
		Delivery Van	2	£275
	11 hp	Open with hs, els	2	£335
		Torpedo with hs, els	4	£350
		Delivery Van	2	£310
	14 hp	Open with hs, els	2	£400
		Torpedo with hs, els	5	£415
		Ambulance with 4 stretchers	2	£405
		Coupé Landaulette	2	£500
		Landaulette	4	£540
1919	10 hp	Open	2–3	£308
		Torpedo	4	£460
	14 hp	Open tourer	5	£456 10s.*
1920	10 hp	Open d	2–3	£480*
		Tourer	4	£530*
		Coupé	2–3	£750
	15.9 hp	Tourer	5	£750
		Saloon	5	£1,010
1921	10 hp	Open d	2–3	£660

YEAR	MODEL	BODY	SEATS	PRICE
		Tourer	4	£700
		Coupé	2–3	£790
	15.9 hp	Tourer	5	£950
		Saloon	5	£1,350
1922	11.4 hp	Open d	2–3	£595
		Tourer	4	£620
		Coupé d	2–3	£725
		Saloon	4	£750
	15.9 hp	Tourer	5	£850
		Saloon	5	£1,200
1923	8 hp	Open 'Chummy'	2–3	£275
	11.4 hp	Open d	2	£510
		Tourer	4	£525
		Coupé d	2	£615
		Saloon	4	£625
		All-Weather	4	£650
	15.9 hp	Tourer	5	£750
		Saloon	5	£985
		Saloon-landaulette	5	£985
1924	8 hp	Open 'Chummy'	2–3	£250
		Open d	2	£250
	11.4 hp	Open d	2	£460
		Tourer	4	£475
		Coupé d	2	£565
		¾-coupé d	2	£600
		Saloon	4	£595
		All-Weather	4	£610
	15.9 hp	Tourer	5	£695
		Saloon	5	£915
		Saloon-landaulette	5	£915
1925	8/18 hp	Open 'Chummy'	2–3	£240
		Open d	2–3	£240
		Saloon	3	£290
	12/25 hp	Open d	2–3	£440
		Tourer	4	£440
		¾-coupé d	2–3	£555
		Saloon	4	£555
		All-Weather	4	£545
	15/40 hp	Tourer	5	£630
		Saloon	5	£845
		Saloon-landaulette	5	£845
1926	9/20 hp	Open d	2–3	£260
		Tourer	4	£260
		Saloon	4	£315
	12/25 hp	Open d	2–3	£440
		Tourer	4–5	£440
		¾-coupé d	2–3	£555
		Saloon	4–5	£555
	15/40 hp	Tourer	5	£645
		Saloon	5	£860
		Saloon-landaulette	5	£860
1927	9/20 hp	Open d	2–3	£260

YEAR	MODEL	BODY	SEATS	PRICE
		Open d fwb after 7.2.27	2–3	£267 7s.
		Tourer	4	£260
		Tourer fwb after 7.2.27	4	£267 7s.
		Saloon	4	£315
		Saloon fwb after 7.2.27	4	£322 7s.
	14/40 hp	Open d	2–3	£460
		Tourer	5	£460
		¾-coupé d	2–3	£575
		Saloon	5	£575
	15/40 hp	Tourer	5	£620
		Saloon	5	£835
		Landaulette	5–7	£835
	20/55 hp	Tourer	5	£725
		Saloon	5	£940
		Landaulette	5–7	£940
		Limousine lwb	7	£1,050
1928	9/20 hp	Open d No. 1	2–3	£250
		Open d No. 2	2–3	£235
		Tourer No. 1	4	£250
		Tourer No. 2	4	£235
		Fabric Saloon No. 1	4	£285
		Saloon No. 1	4	£300
		Saloon No. 2	4	£280
	14/40 hp	Open d No. 1	2–3	£440
		Tourer No. 1	5	£440
		Tourer No. 2	5	£415
		Fabric Saloon No. 1	5	£515
		Saloon No. 1	5	£555
		Saloon No. 2	5	£520
		¾-coupé d	2–3	£555
	20/55 hp	Tourer No. 1	5	£675
		Tourer No. 2	5	£635
		Saloon No. 1	5	£890
		Saloon No. 2	5	£835
		Fabric Saloon No. 1 lwb	5	£860
		Fabric limousine No. 1 lwb	7	£875
		Landaulette No. 1 lwb	7	£995
		Limousine No. 1 lwb	7	£995
		Landaulette No. 2 lwb	7	£935
		Landaulette No. 1	5–7	£900
		Limousine No. 2 lwb	7	£935
1929	9/28 hp	Open d	2–3	£240
		Tourer	4	£240
		Fabric Saloon	4	£280
		Saloon	4	£295
	14/40 hp	Tourer	5	£375
		Fabric Saloon	5	£455
		Saloon	5	£475
	16/50 hp	'Dual Purpose' Tourer	5	£440
		Weymann Fabric Saloon	5	£497
		Saloon	5	£497
	20/65 hp	'Dual Purpose' Tourer	5	£650

YEAR	MODEL	BODY	SEATS	PRICE
		Saloon	5	£845
		Limousine	5–7	£925
		Landaulette	5–7	£925
1930	9/28 hp	Tourer	4	£240
		Fabric Saloon	4	£280
		Saloon	4	£295
	16/50 hp	Imperial Tourer	5	£410
		Tourer	5	£425
		Imperial Saloon	5	£435
		Saloon	5	£465
		Six-light Weymann Fabric Saloon	5	£465
		Four-door Weymann Coupé	5	£475
		Drophead Coupé d	3	£495
	20/65 hp	'Dual Purpose' Tourer	5	£475
		Saloon	5	£525
		Limousine	5–7	£725
		Landaulette	5–7	£725
	'Snipe'	Tourer	5	£495
		Saloon	5	£535
		Six-light Weymann Fabric Saloon	5	£535
		Four-door Weymann Coupé	5	£545
		Drophead Coupé d	3	£565
	Pullman	Landaulette	7	£775
		Limousine	7	£775
		Cabriolet-de-Ville	7	£1,095
1931	16/50 hp	Tourer	5	£395
		Saloon	5	£425
		Saloon sr	5	£435
		Weymann Sports Saloon	5	£460
		Sesame Saloon	5	£475
		Drophead Coupé d	3	£450
	'Snipe'	Tourer	5	£455
		Saloon	5	£485
		Saloon sr	5	£495
		Weymann Sports Saloon	5	£520
		Four-light Saloon	5	£515
		Sesame Saloon	5	£535
		Drophead Coupé d	3	£510
	'Pullman'	Saloon	7	£695
		Limousine	7–8	£735
		Landaulette	7–8	£735
		Cabriolet-de-Ville	7	£995
1932	16/50 hp	Tourer	5	£395
		Saloon	5	£425
		Saloon sr	5	£435
		Drophead Coupé d	3	£450
		Four-light Saloon	5	£455
		Weymann Sports Saloon	5	£460
		Sesame Saloon	5	£475
	'Snipe'	Tourer	5	£435
		Saloon	5	£465
		Saloon sr	5	£475

YEAR	MODEL	BODY	SEATS	PRICE
1932		Drophead Coupé	5	£490
		Four-light Saloon	5	£495
		Four-door Weymann Saloon	5	£500
		Sesame Saloon	5	£515
	'Pullman'	Limousine	7–8	£735
		Landaulette	7–8	£735
		Cabriolet-de-Ville	7	£995

GLOSSARY

B	Beeston
C	Coventry
cch	Cape Cart hood
cs	Canopy and screen
dl	De Luxe
d	Dickey seat
e	Extension
els	Electric lighting and starting
es	Extension and screen
hs	Hood and screen
lwb	Long Wheelbase
R	Royal
RdB	Roi de Belge
re	Rear entrance
se	Side entrance
sr	Sliding roof
ss	Self-starter
swb	Short wheelbase
swt	Spare wheel and tyre
*	Prices rose sharply at this time to £600 for the 14 hp and the 10 hp open 2–3 and £700 for the 10 hp tourer respectively

Production Figures, by Model, 1915–32

10 hp

	Two-seater	Coupé	Four-seater	Chassis	Total
1915	246	–	348	–	594
1916	61	–	70	–	131
1917	19	–	–	–	19
1919	482	3	283	–	768
1920	492	275	519	4	1,290
1921	40	85	119	–	244
	1,340	363	1,339	4	3,046

Chassis Numbers:

Short chassis	Normal chassis
K 953–955	K 1900–1959
K 1100–1299	K 2100–2493
K 1700–1844	K 2495–2615
K 1846	K 2617–2632
K 1848–1899	K 2634–2721
K 3054–4103	K 2722–2887
K 6104–6353	M 5104–5603

11 hp (Separate figures for different body styles not available)

1915	142
1916	50
1917	1
1919	1
	194

Chassis Numbers:
K 1300–1367
K 1369–1494

14 hp (Separate figures for different body styles not available)

1915	234
1916	76
1917	8
1919	107
	425

Chassis Numbers:
H 525–552
H 853–950
K 1500–1652
K 1654–1699
K 2000–2051
K 2053–2099
Exp 394

15.9 hp s.v.

	Tourer	Saloon	Chassis	Landaulette	Coupé	Cabriolet	Two/three seater	Other bodies	Total
1919	3	1	–	–	–	–	–	–	4
1920	549	81	91	13	5	4	10	3	756
1921	361	51	11	9	5	–	–	–	437
1922	256	24	8	10	–	–	–	–	298
1923	5	–	–	–	–	–	–	–	5
	1,174	157	110	32	10	4	10	3	1,500

Chassis Numbers:
M 4104–5103
M 5604–6103

15.9 hp ioe

	Tourer	Saloon	Chassis	Landaulette	Coupé	All-Weather Limousine	Two/three seater	Cabriolet	Total	Chassis Numbers:
1922	67	13	6	7	–	–	–	–	93	M 9604–9999
1923	339	58	17	111	5	3	3	–	537	M 1–104
1924	244	71	11	73	6	7	1	1	417	M 1105–1654
1925	–	–	–	3	–	–	–	–	3	
	650	142	34	194	11	10	4	1	1,050	

11.4 hp

	Tourer		Two/three seater		Coupé		Saloon		All-Weather		Chassis		Total	Chassis Numbers:
	sv	ioe	sv	ioe	sv	ioe	sv	ioe	sv	ioe	sv	ioe		
1921	728	–	507	–	152	–	92	–	5	–	–	–	1,484	M 6354–9103
1922	572	2	428	–	89	2	150	2	21	–	1	–	1,267	M 9104–9603
1923	–	751	1	304	–	123	–	218	4	111	–	11	1,523	M 105–1104
1924	–	677	–	155	–	85	–	208	–	77	–	3	1,205	M 1655–2905
1925	–	11	–	1	–	6	–	–	–	2	–	2	22	
	1,300	1,441	936	460	241	216	242	428	30	190	1	16	5,501	

8 hp

	Chummy	Two-seater	Saloon	Chassis	Special bodies	Total	Chassis Numbers:
1923	870	47	4	9	–	930	L 1–2400
1924	340	481	163	12	3	999	
1925	150	204	108	4	2	468	
1926	1	–	2	–	–	3	
	1,361	732	277	25	5	2,400	

12/25 hp

	Tourer	Two/three seater	Saloon	Coupé	All-Weather	Special bodies	Chassis	Total	Chassis Numbers:
1924	90	41	74	19	8	–	1	233	M 3406–4103
1925	939	199	387	101	40	1	5	1,672	M 10000–10801
1926	542	110	263	54	2	1	9	981	M 11052–11551
1927	68	5	47	–	–	–	–	120	M 11852–12857
	1,639	355	771	174	50	2	15	3,006	

15/40 hp

	Tourer	Saloon	Landaulette	Chassis	Special bodies	Total	Chassis Numbers:
1924	71	28	22	2	1	124	M 2906–3405
1925	373	100	107	12	8	600	M 10802–11051
1926	190	50	65	8	8	321	M 11552–11851
1927	33	10	6	–	1	50	M 13008–13057
1928	4	–	–	–	–	4	
1929	1	–	–	–	–	1	
	672	188	200	22	18	1,100	

9/20 hp

	Tourer	Saloon	Fabric Saloon	Two/three seater	Chassis	Special bodies	Total	Chassis Numbers:
1925	296	49	–	48	–	–	393	L 2401–5850
1926	737	342	–	267	149	2	1,497	
1927	324	216	58	150	65	20	833	
1928	245	201	165	76	1	18	706	
1929	12	4	–	–	–	5	21	
	1,614	812	223	541	215	45	3,450	

20/55 hp

	Tourer	Saloon	Fabric Saloon	Landaulette	Limousine	Fabric Limousine	Special bodies	Chassis	Total	Chassis Numbers:
1926	53	21	–	21	3	–	–	8	106	12352–12357
1927	101	48	1	43	25	4	7	9	238	12858–13001
1928	57	34	3	47	22	7	–	4	174	13567–13866
1929	–	3	–	4	–	–	–	–	7	15617–15690
	211	106	4	115	50	11	7	21	525	15696

14/40 hp

	Tourer	Saloon	Fabric Saloon	Two/three seater	Coupé	Chassis	Special bodies	Total	Chassis Numbers:
1926	92	57	–	4	1	–	–	154	13058–13566
1927	585	466	26	94	61	30	4	1,266	13867–15597
1928	346	256	79	26	25	3	2	737	
1929	28	22	31	1	1	–	–	83	
	1,051	801	136	125	88	33	6	2,240	

9/28 hp

	Tourer	Saloon	Fabric Saloon	Two/three seater	Special bodies	Chassis	Total	Chassis Numbers:
1928	3	2	2	–	–	–	7	L 5851–7095
1929	235	725	161	14	2	4	1,141	L 7098
1930	11	53	35	–	–	–	99	Exp 40, 41
1931	–	–	1	–	–	–	1	
	249	780	199	14	2	4	1,248	

16/50 hp (1929 model)

	Coachbuilt Saloon	Tourer	Weymann Saloon	Sports Coupé	Special bodies	Chassis	Total
1928	169	46	14	–	2	8	239
1929	685	177	109	85	35	20	1,111
1930	1	–	–	–	–	–	1
	855	223	123	85	37	28	1,351

Chassis Numbers:
15817–16816
16917–17166
17267–17366
Exp 37

16/50 hp (1930) model

	Saloon	Tourer	Weymann Six-light Saloon	Weymann Four-door Coupé	Drophead Coupé	Chassis	Total
1929	691	41	71	49	5	14	871
1930	1,460	192	212	164	68	33	2,129
1931	1	1	–	–	–	–	2
	2,152	234	283	213	73	47	3,002

Chassis Numbers:
17367–19366
20367–20866
21477–21976
Exp 42, 43

16/50 hp (1931 model)

	Humber Saloon	Sesame Saloon	Sports Saloon	Four-light saloon	Drophead Coupé	Chassis	Tourer	Total
1930	681	30	63	46	34	36	30	920
1931	1,591	73	156	56	63	53	58	2,050
1932	611	35	102	58	15	23	16	860
	2,883	138	321	160	112	112	104	3,830

Chassis Numbers:
T 22500–25349
T 30001–30980

20/65 hp

	Tourer	Saloon	Landaulette	Limousine	Special bodies	Chassis	Total
1928	7	24	8	8	2	–	49
1929	60	69	40	57	–	8	234
1930	8	5	8	15	–	2	38
1931	–	1	–	–	–	–	1
	75	99	56	80	2	10	322

Chassis Numbers:
15691–15695
15697–15816
16817–16916
17167–17261
17263
Exp 35

'Snipe'

	Saloon	Weymann Saloon	Four-light Saloon	Sports Saloon	Drophead Coupé	Four-door Weymann Coupé	Sesame Saloon	Tourer	Chassis	Total
1929	149	13	–	–	2	15	–	2	6	187
1930	1,184	238	41	72	99	176	28	96	74	2,008
1931	838	–	69	183	38	–	35	52	62	1,277
1932	347	–	31	94	18	–	19	19	36	564
	2,518	251	141	349	157	191	82	169	178	4,036

'Pullman'

	Limousine	Landaulette	Cabriolet-de-Ville	Special bodies	Chassis	Total
1929	5	1	4	2	1	13
1930	257	118	13	4	31	423
1931	181	96	26	–	17	320
1932	104	29	8	–	7	148
	547	244	51	6	56	904

'Snipe' and 'Pullman' Chassis Numbers:
19367–20366
20867–21166
21977–22308
22310–22441
22443–22476
S 26500–27939
S 28400–29140
S 35001–35957
Exp 38, 41, 46, 49

Summary of Production Figures, 1919–32

Year	10 hp	14 hp	15.9 hp	11.4 hp	8 hp	12/25	15/40	9/20	20/55	14/40	9/28	16/50	20/65	Snipe	Pullman	Total
									Model							
1919	768	107	4	–	–	–	–	–	–	–	–	–	–	–	–	879
1920	1,290	–	756	–	–	–	–	–	–	–	–	–	–	–	–	2,046
1921	244	–	437	1,484	–	–	–	–	–	–	–	–	–	–	–	2,165
1922	–	–	391	1,267	–	–	–	–	–	–	–	–	–	–	–	1,658
1923	–	–	542	1,523	930	–	–	–	–	–	–	–	–	–	–	2,995
1924	–	–	417	1,205	999	233	124	–	–	–	–	–	–	–	–	2,978
1925	–	–	3	22	468	1,672	600	393	–	–	–	–	–	–	–	3,158
1926	–	–	–	–	3	981	321	1,497	106	154	–	–	–	–	–	3,062
1927	–	–	–	–	–	120	50	833	238	1,266	–	–	–	–	–	2,507
1928	–	–	–	–	–	–	4	706	174	737	7	239	49	–	–	1,916
1929	–	–	–	–	–	–	1	21	7	83	1,141	1,982	234	187	13	3,669
1930	–	–	–	–	–	–	–	–	–	–	99	3,050	38	2,008	423	5,618
1931	–	–	–	–	–	–	–	–	–	–	1	2,052	1	1,277	320	3,651
1932	–	–	–	–	–	–	–	–	–	–	–	860	–	564	148	1,572
Total	2,302	107	2,550	5,501	2,400	3,006	1,100	3,450	525	2,240	1,248	8,183	322	4,036	904	37,874

Motor Car Production set against Profits and Losses, 1919-32

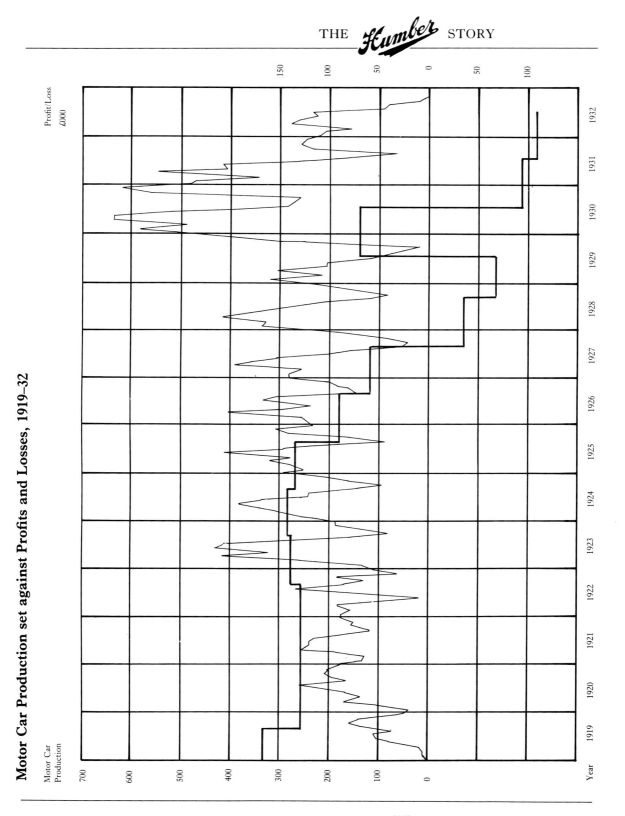

Motor Car
Production

Profit/Loss
£000

700 600 500 400 300 200 100 0

150 100 50 0 50 100

1932 1931 1930 1929 1928 1927 1926 1925 1924 1923 1922 1921 1920 1919   Year

Index

Picture Credits

J. Ahern/D. Irvine, 34; F. Barham, 32, 41; W.E. Barrett, 6 upper; Miss C. Biggs, 65, 73, 91; Dr C.J. Brooks, 7 lower; Mrs E. Chorley, 2; J. Ellis, 113, 114; F.E. Goatcher, 5 upper; M. Hadfield, 17; D. Hales, 37, 49, 58, 62; T. Hayward, 132 lower, 133; R. Howard, 15; F. Howarth, 50, 67, 90; G. Moore, 55; G. Oliver, 134; B. Portas, 2 lower; D. Roberts, 2 upper, 4, 5 lower, 6 lower, 8 upper; Mrs C. Sgonina, 72; Hon. J.A.H. Wallace, 100, 101; The Manx Museum & National Trust, Douglas, 63, 64, 66; The Midland Automobile Club, 74; The National Library of Wales, 40, 54; H.J.F. Thompson, 12; J. Warburton, 53.

All other illustrations can be found in the archives of The Humber Register.